FORMULA ONE ICONS

Written by David Clayton
Designed by Daniel Brawn

ASPEN
BOOKS

© 2023. Published by Aspen Books, an imprint of Pillar Box Red Publishing Ltd. Printed in India.

ISBN: 978-1-914536-73-1

Images © Alamy.

Introduction

Formula 1: the mere mention of this enthralling sport is enough to get the pulse racing as thoughts jump to turbo-powered cars jockeying for position at the start of a Grand Prix before the roaring engines take off around iconic tracks. The pinnacle of motor racing and one of the most prestigious brands in the world, Formula 1 has been in existence for almost 75 years.

The first Formula 1 race was held in 1950, with the organisation uniting the sport to ensure the best Grand Prix in the world all conformed to the same rules and regulations needed to create a World Drivers' Championship.

The glitz and glamour of racing the fastest cars in the world soon ensured that hosting a Formula 1 race was high on the list of any nation with a love of motor sport and a Grand Prix will often attract hundreds of thousands of fans.

Previously, Grand Prix races had taken place all over the world in an unofficial capacity, all under different regulations and with many set in questionable conditions (and therefore unacceptable safety levels).

To meet the strict criteria Formula 1 demanded meant race track owners and Grand Prix organisers had to get their houses in order to ensure they met the necessary standards required, all of which were designed to help protect the safety of drivers and spectators.

Earlier races had been blighted with crashes and, in some instances, large scale loss of life as cars occasionally ploughed into crowds with horrific consequences.

Formula 1 will always be a dangerous sport and more than 50 drivers have lost their lives since 1950 – almost half that total were either British or American – but the continued safety demands of Formula 1 have ensured fatalities have become fewer, both on and off the track.

Formula One Icons dissects the 26 most iconic Formula 1 race circuits across the globe from their inception to creation, tracing their wonderful histories over the years. From epic duels between feuding drivers, to sublimely skilled feats of brilliance, this book captures the very essence of Formula 1, with colourful stories of each circuit featuring at least one memorable win along with the type of car they passed the chequered flag in.

Few sports have attracted the sort of characters that only motor racing seems to produce, with Formula 1 drivers attaining almost rock star like status and superstardom in their homelands. The great and the good are all included from the playboy-style persona of Britain's James Hunt to the revered Brazilian phenomenon that was Ayrton Senna; from the dominance of German machine Michael Schumacher to the heir to his throne, British racing icon Lewis Hamilton and the present day golden boy, Max Verstappen of the Netherlands.

Discover all you need to know about the historic race tracks that have hosted Formula 1 for decades such as Silverstone, Monza, Suzuka, Interlagos and perhaps the glitziest of them all, the street circuit at Monaco, to the newer kids on the block in Abu Dhabi, Singapore, Bahrain, and Saudi Arabia. We also discover the circuits blighted by political interference, financial problems and dogged with continued safety issues that have seen them drop on and off the Formula 1 calendar over the years.

You'll hear the roar of hundreds of thousands of race fans, the revving of these supercar engines and perhaps even smell a whiff of E10 fuel as the pages that follow race by. There's no safety car on this route, so buckle up, shift through the gears, and enjoy learning about the circuits that host the Grand Prix around the world, and the drivers that race at ridiculous speeds with supreme skill and bravery around them.

Hopefully, it won't be a bumpy ride!

CONTENTS

Ayrton Senna
1987

MONACO

NUMBER OF LAPS
78

FIRST GRAND PRIX
1950

CIRCUIT LENGTH
2.074mi

RACE DISTANCE
161.73mi

Narrow, slow and unforgiving yet arguably the race all drivers want to win – there are few Formula 1 destinations with more glamour, history, and romance than the Monaco Grand Prix.

A mainstay of the World Championship since 1950, the Monaco circuit is the embodiment of the sport. The race weaves through the principality, with the playground of the rich and famous providing a glitzy backdrop to a contest that remains the highlight of the Formula 1 calendar.

The famous tunnel, an azure marina full of luxury yachts, and the casinos of Monte Carlo only add to the rich tapestry of this race and give it that extra je ne sais quoi. There are few sights in sport as jaw-dropping as the Formula 1 race through the sun-drenched streets of this French Riviera microstate.

But Monaco is not just about opulence and grandeur, this is a circuit that tests drivers' skills to the limit with the narrow streets, twists and turns and limited space. It is not always a case of who has the fastest car, but more who can rise to the challenge on the day and, crucially, gain the advantage in qualification.

From a driver's point of view, Monaco represents a test of focus like no other

and victory there needs to be earned with intensity and concentration levels higher than anywhere else.

It was Nelson Piquet who claimed that racing at Monaco was the equivalent of 'riding a bicycle around your living room', and Lewis Hamilton, who dreamed of racing the streets of Monte Carlo as a youngster, says that drivers are 'mentally destroyed' for several days after competing there. The hard work is arguably done in the qualifying rounds as overtaking on the Monaco circuit is incredibly difficult. The numerous turns and tight manoeuvres make passing an opponent a rarity, not to mention a dangerous tactic. Monaco has recorded four race fatalities since 1948.

The 78 laps at Monaco equal up to 5,000 gear changes for the driver – that's around 1,000 more than an average circuit and equates to only 42 per cent spent at full throttle which is also the lowest figure of any Formula 1 track.

In the near 100 years that Monaco has hosted races, the course has remained virtually unchanged because the streets of the principality double as the track on race days and only when amends to the roads are made – either to improve daily traffic flow or to upgrade certain sections – does the Monaco circuit

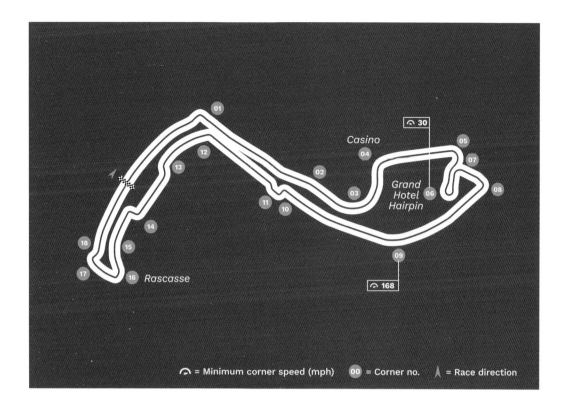

Casino

⌒ 30

Grand
Hotel
Hairpin

Rascasse

⌒ 168

⌒ = Minimum corner speed (mph)   00 = Corner no.   ⋏ = Race direction

change – though these are tweaks at best and few and far between.

At just 2.074 miles (3.337km) Monaco is the shortest track on the F1 calendar – by nearly 0.621 of a mile (1km). And the distance from pole position to the first braking zone is just 125 yards (114 metres), meaning dramatic first sprint passes of the leader are nigh on impossible in lap one.

With only one 1.094 yards (500m) strait to go full throttle and 19 turns, it is very much a stop-start experience from start to finish. Monaco is all about risk and reward, with the winner likely to be the driver who managed to get everything right on the day. To win, it's a case of go big or go home.

The circuit's complexity means there are numerous slow- to medium-speed corners, with the Grand Hotel Hairpin bend the slowest in Formula 1.

The famous tunnel section first appeared in 1973, adding yet more mystique to the circuit, as do the corners at Swimming Pool Chicane,

Tabac, Portier and Casino Square.

Cars are often modified for Monaco, which is also notoriously bumpy due to the network of streets used for public transport outside of Formula 1 competition.

"Mastering a lap in Monaco, of course you've got to have a light and nimble car, you've got to have great downforce, you've got to have the right power to weight ratio, you've got to have the right track position, clean air in front of you, commitment, you've got to be willing to touch the barriers," claims seven-time world champion Lewis Hamilton.

The legendary Ayrton Senna relished racing at Monaco, winning the race a record six times – fitting that the enigmatic Brazilian should display his greatest feats in such an iconic setting.

Put simply, Monaco is unique and Formula 1 would be a duller sport without it. It remains the jewel of the Formula 1 calendar.

BAHRAIN

Felipe Massa
2007

SAKHIR

NUMBER OF LAPS

57

FIRST GRAND PRIX

2004

CIRCUIT LENGTH

3.362mi

RACE DISTANCE

191.53mi

Bahrain sits in the Persian Gulf surrounded by sea and blessed with year-round sunshine.

It is also home to the Bahrain International Circuit, set in the desert area of Sakhir in the south of the island, and was the first circuit to host Formula 1 in the Middle East upon its completion back in 2004.

Designed by the renowned Hermann Tilke – the German architect behind the Sepang International Circuit in Malaysia, Sakhir comprises of five tracks and incorporates many aspects of Bahraini and Middle Eastern culture.

With only 18 months for construction, it was a race against time to get the track ready for the inaugural 2004 race, particularly with Egypt, UAE and Lebanon competing to become the Middle East Formula 1 flagbearer.

But at a cost of approximately £122.4 million ($150million), the circuit met its deadline and, as a result, joined the elite group of worldwide Grand Prix tracks – much to the pride of a Kingdom of fewer than 1.5 milllion people.

The foundations of the track were anything but local to the island, however. They were shipped to Bahrain from a quarry in Shropshire, England, with the track

surface ultimately winning worldwide acclaim for the grip it allows drivers.

Being set on an island that is just 30 miles long (48.3km) and 10 miles wide (16.1km), the winds off the ocean and the desert landscape meant sand presented a potentially unique and dangerous problem for planners to solve.

The prospect of sand being blown across the track during a Grand Prix would present major issues for drivers and their high performing cars.

Ingeniously, the decision was taken to spray adhesive on the sand surrounding Sakhir to ensure this would never be an issue – it was a sizeable task, but like all hurdles presented, it was dealt with expertly and without fuss.

In April 2004, Michael Schumacher was first to the chequered flag at the inaugural Formula 1 race to be held in Bahrain, but there would be changes made to the circuit ahead of the 2005 race due to several teething issues that had been perhaps papered over in order to comply with the initial and binding contract deadline of 12 months prior.

It was decided that the track needed realignment at turn four, resulting in a decrease of 16.4 feet (five metres)

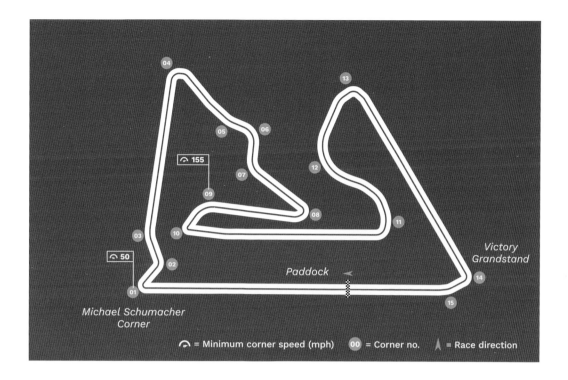

The diagram shows:

- 04
- 13
- 05
- 06
- ⌒ 155
- 12
- 07
- 09
- 08
- 11
- 03
- 10
- Victory Grandstand
- ⌒ 50
- 02
- Paddock
- 14
- 01
- 15
- Michael Schumacher Corner

⌒ = Minimum corner speed (mph)   00 = Corner no.   ⋀ = Race direction

in total by the time the second Formula 1 battle commenced.

The tweaks resulted in a track that is popular with drivers and constructors alike and just three years into existence, Sakhir became the first Grand Prix circuit to be awarded the FIA Institute Centre of Excellence award for its superb safety record and overall facilities.

The legacy of Formula 1 legend Michael Schumacher and that first chequered flag back in 2004 was not forgotten by the people of Bahrain, and after suffering a near-fatal skiing accident in 2013, the first corner of Sakhir was renamed in honour of the German driver in time for the 2014 race.

Pedro de la Rosa holds the lap record of 1:31.447 set in 2005, but track amends thereafter mean the five-times Bahrain winner Lewis Hamilton currently holds the track record of 1:27.264.

Though Hamilton's five wins is the most to date, Sebastian Vettel has four wins, Fernando Alonso three and Felipe Massa won his two back-to-back titles in 2007 and 2008.

The 2007 triumph saw the Brazilian at his very best, dominating the race in his Ferrari and swatting off rivals when they had the temerity to briefly overtake.

Massa led from pole to lap 21 when Kimi Räikkönen wrestled the advantage to lead for the next two circuits. Massa eased past the Finn and would continue to lead the race for the next 16 laps.

The emerging talent that was Lewis Hamilton, full of vigour, adrenaline and youthful exuberance, pushed Massa all the way and on lap 41, passed the Brazilian and led for three laps – but Massa bided his time, regained the advantage on lap 45 and held out to the chequered flag with a masterclass of controlled driving in his Ferrari F2007 car. It also completed the first hat-trick of Formula 1 wins of his career.

The course is 3.362 miles (5.412km) over 57 laps and is among the most respected and popular destinations on the Formula 1 calendar.

SAUDI
ARABIA

Lewis Hamilton

2021

JEDDAH

NUMBER OF LAPS
50

FIRST GRAND PRIX
2021

CIRCUIT LENGTH
3.836mi

RACE DISTANCE
191.66mi

One of the new kids on the block, the Jeddah Corniche Circuit is unique in many ways.

Spectacular, innovative and sleek, Jeddah was designed to be fast, challenging, and full of thrills and spills, with the backdrop of an 18.6 mile (30km) coastal resort on the Red Sea. Jeddah demanded a track that appealed to constructors and drivers alike, so, using the expertise of the Tilke company, the circuit was designed with the sizeable input of the Formula Motorsports team who utilised Google Earth when first researching what was possible.

Like Monaco, Jeddah is a street circuit. Also, like Monaco, it is situated in salubrious surroundings, with a backdrop of luxury hotels, the ocean and sky scrapers.

But that's largely where the comparison ends. The gruelling focus needed in Monaco, with it's 90-degree turns and limited opportunities to shift through the gears, cannot be said of Jeddah where, with a blank canvas, the design is a long, narrow loop around the city that is guaranteed to bring drama and excitement in equal measure.

A temporary street circuit, Jeddah also has some permanent sections that were

evident in its first F1 race – the 2021 Saudi Arabian Grand Prix – and it became the third Middle Eastern destination on the Formula 1 calendar after Bahrain and Abu Dhabi and, like its desert-dominated cousins, it hosts a floodlit race.

At 3.836 miles (6.174km) Jeddah is the second-longest circuit in Formula 1 and has three marked possible DRS zones.

Jeddah was designed for speed and has quickly moved to being second-fastest on the Formula 1 track list behind Monza, with estimates that average speeds will be as much as 157mph (252kmh). But while it isn't the fastest overall, it is by far the quickest street circuit.

With 27 corners to tackle, it has more than any other track, with the majority along the sweeping Jeddah waterfront section.

The 2021 inaugural race would not disappoint, with Lewis Hamilton writing his name into the Jeddah history books by being first across the finish line after a thrilling 50 laps, which equated to 191.7 miles (308.45km) in total distance.

Hamilton posted the lap record of 1:30.734 on his way to the chequered flag in his Mercedes W12, but the race was not without incident, with crashes, collisions and restarts – not to mention

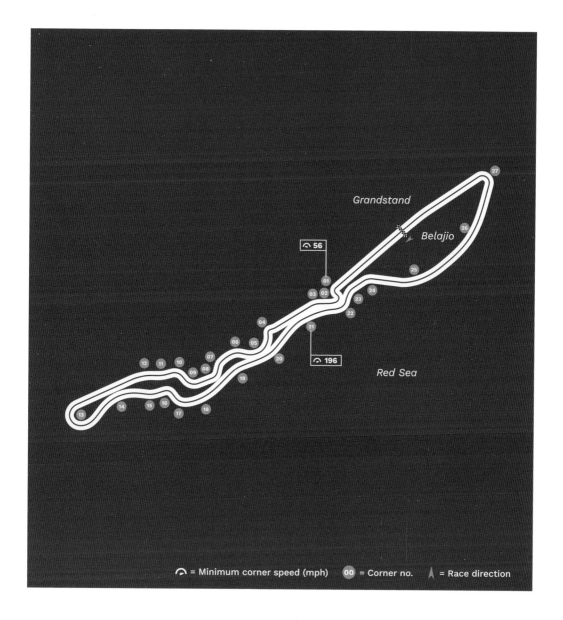

Grandstand

Belajio

⌒ 56

Red Sea

⌒ = Minimum corner speed (mph)　　00 = Corner no.　　⋀ = Race direction

the fascinating subplot of Hamilton and rival Max Verstappen continuing to court controversy as both drivers pushed the boundaries in a bid to be world champions, and in Verstappen's case, pushing the boundaries too far.

The Dutch driver's illegal overtaking of Hamilton on lap 37 led to the race stewards ordering him to allow Hamilton to pass – but with Hamilton unaware of this, Verstappen's sudden and dramatic drop in speed caused him to run into the rear of Verstappen's car, with both drivers suffering damage as a result.

Hamilton recovered sufficiently and as the pair continued to exchange metaphorical blows, on lap 43 Hamilton seized back the lead and saw out the remaining seven laps in front, banking maximum points in the process to draw equal first in the championship with Verstappen, who had also been given a 10-second time penalty. It all added to the excitement and drama Jeddah had provided at the first time of asking, and with more than 143,000 people attending the three-day weekend, it was considered a resounding success and a welcome addition to the calendar.

AUSTRALIA

Jenson Button
2009

MELBOURNE

NUMBER OF LAPS
58

FIRST GRAND PRIX
1996

CIRCUIT LENGTH
3.279mi

RACE DISTANCE
190.21mi

Fast and with a reputation of being an easier ride than most, Melbourne's Albert Park Circuit remains a popular destination for Formula 1 drivers and fans alike.

A race track had been mooted since the 1930s without success until the necessary amendments to the existing roads were made and the 1953 Australian Grand Prix was finally held there.

The circuit closed five years later, and numerous cities would hold major races in the years that followed.

Adelaide hosted Formula 1 on its street circuit for a decade (1985-1995) before plans were announced to move the Australian Grand Prix to Melbourne.

Driven by the disappointment of missing out on hosting the 1996 Summer Olympics, a mixture of private equity and government funding made it possible to create the semi-permanent Albert Park Circuit, though local protesters in the city were against the plan, claiming it would turn the park into a "private playground" for one week of each year.

However, the economic benefits were deemed to far outweigh the negatives and the project got the green light from government, much to the chagrin of Adelaide.

In 1996, the Albert Park Circuit was completed, a deal agreed with Formula 1 boss Bernie Ecclestone, and Great Britain's Damon Hill was the first winner at the new venue.

The Formula 1 Australian Grand Prix has been held at Albert Park ever since. The track is housed within the surrounds of arguably one of the city's most beautiful parks and the circuit is made up of the public roads adjacent to Albert Park Lake.

Turning the gentle lake surrounds into a major race venue that can accommodate hundreds of thousands of fans takes several months – indeed, the change is so dramatic that Albert Park is almost unrecognisable.

Measuring 3.279 miles (5.278km) in length, the Melbourne Grand Prix Circuit – to give it its official name – consists of 58 laps with a total distance covered of 190.21 miles (306.12km) with turns and grandstands named after racing legends such as Stirling Moss, Jack Brabham, Ayrton Senna, Alain Prost and Nelson Piquet among others.

One unique aspect of Albert Park is that drivers are never more than a stone's throw from water, with the park's magnificent lake providing the central focus of the circuit. However, hidden behind barricades,

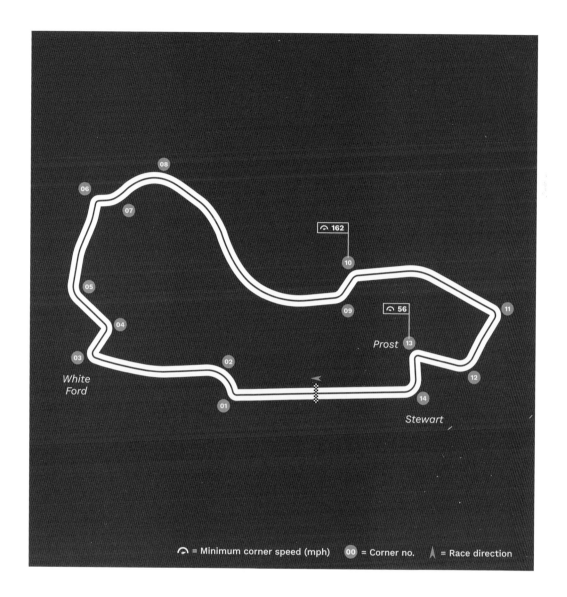

162

56

Prost 13

White
Ford

Stewart

⌒ = Minimum corner speed (mph)   00 = Corner no.   ⌁ = Race direction

high fencing and media equipment, the drivers would never know the 1.1 m² (0.49km²) body of water was there.

There have been many epic races in Melbourne, which regularly attracts more than 450,000 people over race weekend, but Jenson Button's victory in 2009 in his Mercedes FO 108W is fondly remembered, with the British driver leading from the very first lap to secure one of 15 career wins, and that year his only World Championship triumph.

It was quite a start for the Brawn-Mercedes team, with Rubens Barrichello ensuring they had a first and second

place on the podium in their debut race for the new constructor.

It was one of three wins for Button at Albert Park, with Michael Schumacher holding the record for the most victories (four).

Melbourne has been the first race on the Formula 1 calendar on numerous occasions, though it has been less prevalent in recent years with new circuits offering the tour a wider variety of options.

It remains a popular destination that rightly holds an esteemed place in Formula 1 history.

ITALY

Lewis Hamilton
2020

IMOLA

NUMBER OF LAPS

63

FIRST GRAND PRIX

1980

CIRCUIT LENGTH

3.050mi

RACE DISTANCE

192.03mi

The Emilia-Romagna Grand Prix, formerly known as the San Marino Grand Prix (1981-2006) – is better known simply as 'Imola' – though it is, in effect, one of two Italian Grand Prix races.

Situated some 25 miles (40km) east of the Italian city of Bologna, Imola is unique in a number of ways, but the main difference to many of the other Formula 1 circuits is that the race runs anti-clockwise – one of only a handful to do so across the globe.

At 63 laps, the 3.05 mile (4.909km) track has seen some epic battles down the years – as well as more than its fair share of horror – and it is also the spiritual home of Scuderia Ferrari, with the Ferrari family's influence abundant at Imola.

Though the iconic Monza could be argued to be Italy's premier race circuit, Imola has fought to take that crown, emerging in various guises over the years.

It began life as a basic designed track in the early 1950s with no chicanes, some gentle bends and straights, and remained so until 1972.

The first Formula 1 race was hosted in 1963, though Jim Clark's victory for Lotus did not count towards the World Championship and a similar

non-points event was held in 1979, with Niki Lauda taking the chequered flag for Brabham-Alfa Romeo.

Imola would have to wait more than 12 months before it became an official Formula 1 venue, hosting the 1980 Italian Grand Prix for the first time and becoming the first circuit in Italy to hold the race outside Monza for 32 years – with Nelson Piquet finishing first on the podium.

The popularity of Imola was immediate, but rather than lose the equally popular Monza off the Formula 1 roster, a deal to accommodate both was agreed, with Imola instead becoming the San Marino Grand Prix, with the mountainous microstate situated a little over an hour south east of the Italian city.

It would remain on the Formula 1 calendar until 2006, though the tragic events of the 1994 race resulted in major safety improvements at Imola.

Over two horrific days, both Austrian driver Roland Ratzenberger and the revered Brazilian legend Ayrton Senna were killed as results of catastrophic crashes on the circuit, leaving the world of Formula 1 motor racing in a state of shock.

Immediate redesigns to reduce danger

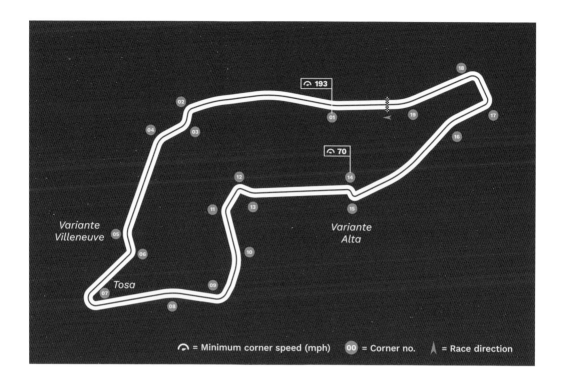

○ 193

○ 70

02
01
19
18
17
16
04
03
12
14
11
13
15
05
06
10
Variante
Villeneuve
Variante
Alta
Tosa
09
07
08

○ = Minimum corner speed (mph)   00 = Corner no.   ▲ = Race direction

and slow certain sections of the track down dramatically were made, though few could forget the events of '94.

Indeed, lessons learned and safety improvements as a result of this double tragedy would be implemented throughout Formula 1 venues thereafter and undoubtedly saved many lives as a result.

But Imola's issues weren't fully over. There were still concerns and areas that many drivers weren't happy with and after a number of issues with the Variante Alta (high variant) chicane in particular, Imola was removed from Formula 1's 2007 calendar.

Renovation and improvements continued over the next few years, until the track was deemed safe enough for Formula 1 cars again in 2011, passing crucial safety tests.

Keen to become a Formula 1 destination once more, Imola looked to have secured a return when Monza's contract ended in 2016. Imola was scheduled for a slot on the 2017 calendar, but Monza later announced they had secured a deal to continue

hosting the Italian Grand Prix leaving Imola no option but to legally challenge the deal.

Eventually Imola's legal representatives dropped the case, perhaps sensing a protracted and expensive battle through the courts, and instead bided their time.

An unexpected opportunity arose in 2020, when Imola stepped in to fill the void left by the Chinese Grand Prix, cancelled as a result of the pandemic.

The first race at Imola – renamed officially as the Emilia Romagna Grand Prix – for 14 years did not disappoint, with a race full of drama, delays and tactical driving won by Lewis Hamilton, who crossed the line in his Mercedes-AMG F1 W11 EQ Performance car almost six seconds ahead of Mercedes team-mate Valtteri Bottas to secure a seventh consecutive constructors' championship for Mercedes as a result.

Formula 1 had finally returned to the historic track and further races were held in 2021 and 2022, with Imola guaranteed as a venue until at least 2025.

SPAIN

Nigel Mansell
1992

BARCELONA

Circuit de Barcelona-Catalunya

NUMBER OF LAPS
66

FIRST GRAND PRIX
1991

CIRCUIT LENGTH
2.904mi

RACE DISTANCE
191.64mi

One of Formula 1's most popular destinations, the Circuit de Barcelona-Catalunya, Barcelona has been hosting the Spanish Grand Prix since 1991.

Prior to that, races had been held at Pedralbes, Jarama, Montjuïc and Jerez, with the race being one of the oldest in the world, having first been held in 1913.

With Barcelona awarded the 1992 Summer Olympics, the opportunity to give Spain a brand new and permanent home for its Grand Prix was never more appealing.

A combination of the Catalan Government, Montmeló Town Council and the Royal Automobile Club of Catalonia pooled their knowledge and financial muscle to create a circuit that is often described as an 'all-rounder', bringing different aspects of race skills into play on its 2.904 mile (4.675km) track that features 16 turns and is contested over 66 laps.

Located in the small municipality of Montmeló in Barcelona, the first Grand Prix was held on 29 September 1991, barely three weeks after its official opening. With a capacity of 140,700, Circuit de Barcelona-Catalunya made an explosive debut on the Formula 1 tour with the inaugural race proving to be a thrilling affair.

The 14th of 16 Formula 1 Grand Prix races, Great Britain's Nigel Mansell and Brazil's Ayrton Senna were battling for the championship throughout a memorable season, with Senna winning six races and Mansell four.

The British driver had been dealt a major blow in the race before, being disqualified in the Portuguese Grand Prix after a disastrous pit stop saw him drive away with a wheel not properly attached.

It meant he was 24 points behind Senna with only three races remaining and Mansell, driving a Renault RS3C RS4 V10, simply had to win in Spain – and he did exactly that to keep his title hopes alive with a stunning drive that at one stage saw him racing Senna side-by-side down the back straight, much to the delight of the fans in attendance.

Senna, knowing he could win the title without finishing first in any of the remaining races, was eventually passed by Mansell who went on to win the race and reduce the deficit to 16 points with two races to go. Senna, however, would ultimately win the World Drivers' Championship by 24 points.

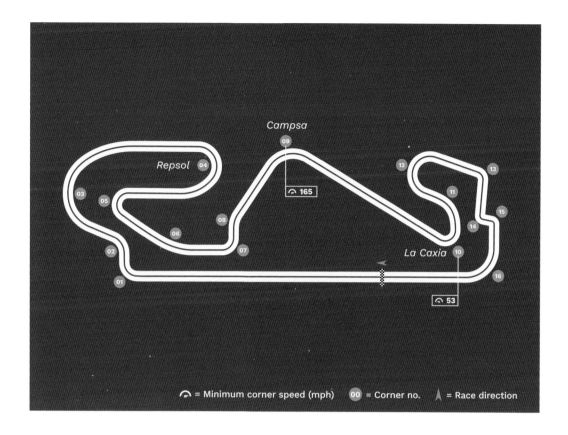

Campsa

Repsol 04

09

165

12

13

03

05

11

08

15

06

14

02

07

La Caxia 10

16

01

53

⌒ = Minimum corner speed (mph)   00 = Corner no.   ⋀ = Race direction

Over the years, Ferrari (eight wins) have proved the most successful constructor, with Mercedes (seven) and Williams (six) also performing well in Barcelona.

The 1991 race became an instant classic and had proved a wonderful introduction for race fans and drivers at the new track. The Circuit de Barcelona-Catalunya has hosted the Spanish Grand Prix ever since as well as numerous other major motor sport championship races.

With no local hero to support, the Spanish Grand Prix in Barcelona initially struggled to attract large crowds, and it wasn't until the emergence of Fernando Alonso that attendances dramatically improved.

During its 31 years of hosting Formula 1, British and German drivers have won more than any other nationality, with 10 for Britain and eight for Germany – Michael Schumacher and Lewis

Hamilton have each won six races there – Spanish icon Fernando Alonso has recorded just two wins on home soil.

One of Formula 1's main testing tracks for many years, there has been criticism that driver familiarity with the Spanish Grand Prix circuit has reduced excitement in more recent times and amendments have been made to offer greater opportunities to overtake.

Shifting wind conditions can also be an issue for the aerodynamics of Formula 1 cars, with planning difficult from one session to the next due to the ever-changing winds that were blamed for Fernando Alonso's 2015 testing accident.

Numerous chicane and hairpin remodelling projects have been undertaken to improve safety and Barcelona remains a highlight on the Formula 1 calendar.

Azerbaijan

Valtteri Bottas
2019

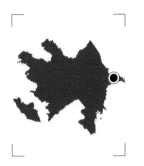

NUMBER OF LAPS	FIRST GRAND PRIX	CIRCUIT LENGTH	RACE DISTANCE
51	**2016**	**3.730mi**	**190.17mi**

It's fair to say that when people talk of the glamour and glitz of Formula 1 racing, Azerbaijan isn't the first destination that springs to mind.

With a population of less than 11 milion, the former Soviet Union republic of Azerbaijan hosts a race that is one of the latest additions to the Formula 1 calendar. The first race was held in 2016 under the generic title 'European Grand Prix' as the capital city of Baku joined the select group of street circuits that includes Canada, Australia, Monaco, and Singapore.

Won by Nico Rosberg, that was the precursor to Azerbaijan earning its own Formula 1 slot.

Red Bull's Daniel Ricciardo would take the chequered flag in the first officially named Azerbaijan Grand Prix in 2017 – one of three Red Bull triumphs to date in a race no driver has won more than once.

Set on an unusually designed track that, aerially, resembles half circular and half rectangular, the temporary circuit – designed by Hermann Tilke – measures 3.730 miles (6.003km) and is fought over 51 laps.

With the Baku city walls and impressive skyscrapers forming a dramatic backdrop, cars race through the streets, with

several sharp turns along the way.

Initial safety concerns were raised regarding pit entries and loose kerbs before the issues were dealt with.

With plenty of twists and turns along the way, the Baku City Circuit also has a long main straight that runs along the city's shoreline, creating a "slipstreaming mecca" that allows as many as three cars to race side-by-side. The width throughout varies from wide 42.7 feet (13 metres) to narrow 25 feet (7.6 metres) and there are a total of 20 turns to handle on each lap, making it a mentally exhausting task to complete without issue.

The slower sections include loops around Baku's old town of İcheri Sheher, taking drivers past the spectacular medieval city walls – an area that requires complete focus and concentration to negotiate where the slightest error can be costly.

With the track running through part of a UNESCO World Heritage Site, some of the area's cobbled streets needed to have an asphalt covering for cars to pass safely over – cobbles and Formula 1 cars do not go together!

Though there have only been a handful of races in Baku, the 2019 Grand Prix proved an exciting battle between Mercedes team-

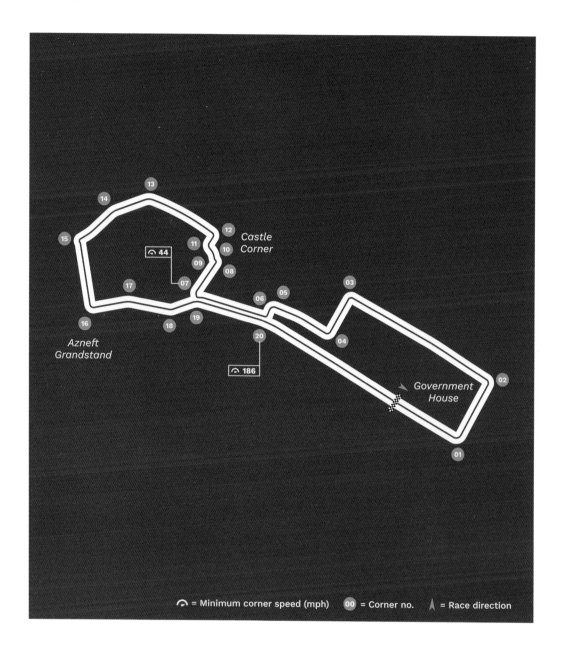

13

14

15

12

Castle
Corner

11

10

⌒ 44

09

08

17

07

16

18

19

Azneft
Grandstand

20

⌒ 186

03

06

05

04

Government
House

02

01

⌒ = Minimum corner speed (mph)   00 = Corner no.   ⋀ = Race direction

mates Lewis Hamilton and Valtteri Bottas.

The pair had finished one-two in the three previous races and would repeat the feat again, with Finnish driver Bottas taking the chequered flag 1.52 seconds ahead of his British team-mate in his Mercedes AMG F1 W10 EQ Power+ car.

Bottas started on pole and had to fend off Hamilton's attempts to pass, eventually crossing the line for only his fifth F1 victory at that stage, and

one that put him one point ahead of Hamilton in the Drivers' Championship.

The COVID-19 pandemic ensured Baku's 2020 Grand Prix was cancelled, and a year later it was held without spectators, making the empty streets an eerie backdrop as the cars circled the city.

Fans made a welcome return to the 2022 race and F1 is guaranteed at the Baku City Circuit until at least 2024.

CA
NA
DA

Gilles Villeneuve
1978

MONTRÉAL

NUMBER OF LAPS

70

FIRST GRAND PRIX

1978

CIRCUIT LENGTH

2.709mi

RACE DISTANCE

189.68mi

The Canadian Grand Prix has been held at the Circuit Gilles-Villeneuve in Montréal for more than 44 years, making it one of Formula 1's best known and longest-serving circuits.

A fast – though stop-start – course with lots of sharp braking chicanes and The Hairpin ('L'Epingle') where there is rarely a dull moment, it remains a favourite destination for drivers.

The first Grand Prix there was held in 1978 and would be won in dramatic style by Canadian icon and local Quebecer Gilles Villeneuve, making the annual Grand Prix an instant hit with race fans in North America.

Originally raced in the damper climate of September, it later moved to June to ensure the best racing conditions for drivers and fans.

The Canadian Grand Prix was first held in 1967 and for the next decade it was held in Toronto and later Quebec, before a more permanent venue was agreed in Montréal .

Circuit Gilles-Villeneuve was originally christened the Île Notre-Dame Circuit, as the man-made Notre Dame Island was the obvious location for a race track.

Notre Dame Island had been specially constructed for Expo '67, a fair to celebrate Canada's centenary. It was set in the St. Lawrence River and the layout was perfect to create a dedicated motor circuit.

But the Canadian Grand Prix would become one of the calendar's most unpredictable races, and over the years has undergone many changes that has reduced both the length and number of turns.

It's a circuit few have mastered and some of its features – particularly the notorious Quebec Wall outside the exit of the final chicane – has ended the race for many high-profile drivers.

So many, in fact, that today the wall has been renamed the 'Wall of Champions' – ironic given that so many had collisions with it that it put a dent not only in their high-powered cars, but their World Drivers' Championship hopes, too!

Safety amends have been made all over the track, but especially after the double-tragedy of 1994 when both Ayrton Senna and Roland Ratzenberger were involved in fatal collisions that made the sport look long and hard at the demands it was placing on the drivers and their cars.

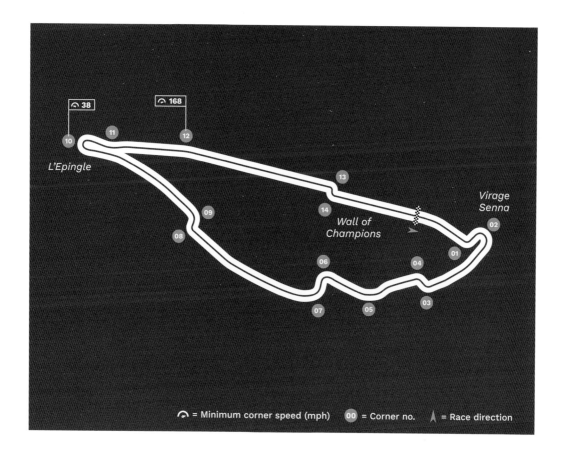

With a capacity of 100,000, the Circuit Gilles-Villeneuve today measures 2.710 miles (4.361km) and has 14 turns – six fewer than the 20 of 1994-95.

For various reasons, the 70-lap race has had one or two 'gap years', not featuring on the Formula 1 calendar in 1987, 2009, 2020 or 2021.

The circuit has proved a particular favourite of Michael Schumacher and Lewis Hamilton, who have both won seven times, while Ferrari (14) and McLaren (13) are the constructors who have dominated over the years.

But few will ever forget that inaugural race of 1978 when Gilles Villeneuve took the chequered flag in front of an ecstatic home crowd. The largely French-speaking province would likely have been satisfied had

Frenchman Jean-Pierre Jarier come first. He made a magnificent attempt and had to battle various engine issues after starting on pole in his Lotus, but saw his race end due to an oil leak on lap 49, allowing Villeneuve to take command in his Ferrari 312T3.

Tragically, Villeneuve would die in a fatal crash just four years later and Île Notre-Dame Circuit was renamed in his honour in time for the 1982 race. Villeneuve remains the only Canadian to have won the race on home turf, though his son Jacques Villeneuve became world champion in 1997 and remains the first – and, to date, only – Canadian to do so.

The circuit is a fitting legacy for a family who have done so much to put F1 on the map in North America.

UNITED KINGDOM

Jackie Stewart
1969

TOWCESTER

NUMBER OF LAPS

52

FIRST GRAND PRIX

1950

CIRCUIT LENGTH

3.660mi

RACE DISTANCE

190.26mi

One of Formula 1's most iconic destinations, Silverstone, home of the British Grand Prix, can justifiably claim to be one of the sport's most famous and loved race tracks.

Located in the leafy Northamptonshire countryside, on the border of Buckinghamshire, Silverstone has been hosting Formula 1 since 1948 and it was the venue for the very first World Championship of Drivers race in 1950.

The British Grand Prix was not exclusively held at Silverstone initially, with circuits at Aintree and Brands Hatch also hosting the event on a rotational basis between 1955 and 1986.

From 1987 onwards, however, Silverstone has been the permanent home of British Formula 1.

Built on the site of a former RAF bomber base, the land around Silverstone was perfect for a race track, with three long runways already in existence and the terrain being flat and open for miles around.

Indeed, the first amateur event held there was fought out on a circuit that used the runways' wide and flat expanse as

the perfect surface for high speed races – though initial meetings had to avoid the sheep that grazed the land freely!

Eventually, the perimeter track around the base was used, and this became the basis of the circuit we see today, with the first official race held in 1948 – though there have been numerous improvements made over the years and a major redesign was undertaken between 1990 and 1991 to make Silverstone an 'ultra-fast track'. Silverstone's long and colourful history has seen many classic battles take place, with the 1969 British Grand Prix most certainly among them.

Austria's Jochen Rindt started on pole, but Britain's Jackie Stewart – winner of four of the previous five races – was determined to give the home fans a victory.

He and Rindt battled gamely throughout, until Stewart spotted a fault on his rival's car, signalled to him that he had an issue, and as Rindt could see the end plate on his rear wing was insecure in his rear-view mirror, he was forced to take a pit stop.

Stewart, in his Matra MS80 and on his way to the first of three world titles, took complete command as a result and was able to lap the entire field

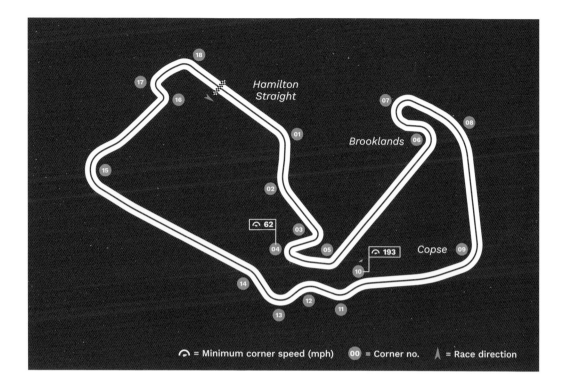

ensuring that while he completed the full 84 laps, the nearest of his challengers saw their race end on lap 83.

Of the constructors, Ferrari have always performed well at Silverstone, and the British Grand Prix in general, taking 18 victories overall, though it's worth noting that there have been 24 British constructor wins if McLaren's 14 and Williams' 10 triumphs are combined.

While Stewart's 1969 race win was over 84 laps, the track today is raced over 3.660 miles (5.981km) and a significantly lower total of 52 laps.

Between 1987 and 1990, steps were taken to slow the circuit down as the evermore powerful cars were simply going too fast.

Between 1991 and 1993, major changes were made again with almost half of the Silverstone track redesigned, which left many feeling it lost some of its character and charm as a result.

Silverstone has seen many British winners, none more than Lewis Hamilton who has clocked up a record eight victories going into 2023.

It regularly attracts vast crowds in excess of 400,000 over the three-day event weekend and clearly, with 24 track wins by British drivers, the patriotism, noise and thousands of Union Jack flags waving inspires home drivers to dig that little bit deeper.

Despite its history and popularity, there have been several occasions when Silverstone looked to have held its last British Grand Prix over the years, but each time – either due to issues with prospective other venues, last-gasp agreements or contractual issues – the race has remained at Silverstone and will do so until 2024 at least.

Silverstone also has an excellent safety record, with no driver fatalities recorded during a British Grand Prix at the circuit in its 74-year existence – and long may that continue.

AUSTRIA

Alain Prost
1985

SPIELBERG

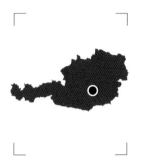

NUMBER OF LAPS

71

FIRST GRAND PRIX

1970

CIRCUIT LENGTH

2.683mi

RACE DISTANCE

190.42mi

When it comes to spectacular backdrops and breathtaking scenery, the Red Bull Ring sits among the most picturesque on the Formula 1 calendar.

Set in Spielberg in Austria, the race track was first created in 1969, replacing the unpopular and – in truth – unloved Zeltweg airfield circuit just a stone's throw away.

The uninspiring Zeltweg had hosted races between 1958 and 1968 but was both flat and bumpy with parallel stretches of runway that gave away the track's original purpose.

Known as the Österreichring – Austrian Circuit – it would become the home of the Austrian Grand Prix from 1970 through to 1987.

The new track was a breath of fresh air, set in the freshest of mountain air and would quickly become a 'drivers circuit' – a destination where a thirst for speed was quenched.

Österreichring had many unique features, with narrow sections of just 33 feet (10 metres) in places and elevation shifts of 213 feet (65 metres) from the lowest to the highest points on the track. It was also incredibly fast, and with that came excessive demands on engines

and tyres, making the circuit dangerous in parts with speeds of up to 214mph (344kph) recorded as far back as 1986.

With uphill right-hand turns, the downhill ride can be exhilarating thanks to a series of quick corners and four long sections where drivers can put the pedal to the metal, so to speak.

There were many classic battles on the track – as well as crashes and mishaps aplenty – with the 1985 Grand Prix seeing Alain Prost and his great rival Ayrton Senna going head to head.

In what was Austria's 25th Formula 1 battle, Prost would control the race from pole and finish 30 seconds ahead of Senna as he recorded his fourth win of the season in his McLaren MP4/2B.

But fatal crashes, accidents and even a deer being struck on the track proved too much for F1 organisers who had no stomach for the unpredictable races in Spielberg, which had given a number of relatively unknown drivers completely unexpected victories.

In 1987, Österreichring disappeared off the calendar for a decade, as improvements and various changes were made under the tutelage of Hermann Tilke, including shortening the track, re-emerging on the

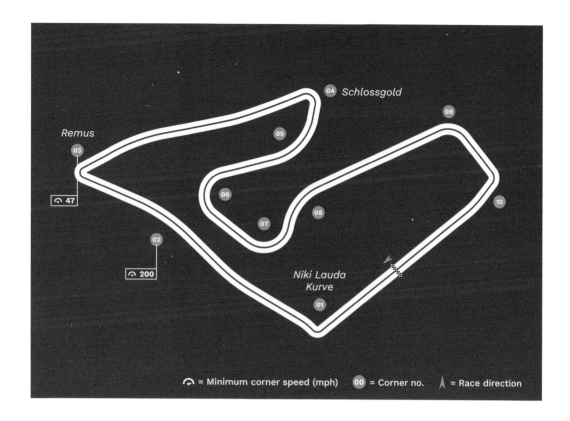

Schlossgold
Remus
Niki Lauda Kurve

04 Schlossgold
09
05
Remus
03
06
47
10
02
08
07
200
01

= Minimum corner speed (mph)   00 = Corner no.   = Race direction

F1 tour in 1997 for another six years.

But the circuit – also known at this point as the A-1 Ring – was dated and needed substantial changes to bring it in line with the standards demanded by Formula 1, so after the 2003 race, the Österreichring once again fell off the calendar.

Plans were drawn up to extend the circuit, and the grandstand and pits were demolished as part of the rebuild, but the project proved extremely expensive, and work ceased for a number of years, leaving many wondering if it would ever host F1 again.

Fortunately, Austrian billionaire Dietrich Mateschitz – co-founder and major shareholder of energy drink company Red Bull – stepped in to supply the necessary funding to get the track back up to scratch and bring F1 back to Spielberg. Initial plans for a £500million ($610 million) overhaul including a museum, race school and a home for Mateschitz's aircraft collection met resistance and

work was halted for several years before a more palatable plan was resubmitted and approved by local authorities.

Rebranded and renamed, the Österreichring became the Red Bull Ring and was reopened for business in May 2011, though F1 would not return until 2014 where it has remained on the calendar ever since.

With a circuit length of 2.683 miles (4.318km) and a 71-lap course, the Red Bull Ring is one of the shorter circuits on the F1 calendar, but it packs a real punch despite its size and can house as many as 105,000 people.

It remains a circuit few have mastered over the years – by 2022 no driver had won there more than three times and the constructors win totals has a very even spread with Ferrari's seven triumphs leading the way – perhaps highlighting the undoubted charm of this race among the mountains.

France

Keke Rosberg
1985

LE CASTELLET

NUMBER OF LAPS

53

FIRST GRAND PRIX

1971

CIRCUIT LENGTH

3.630mi

RACE DISTANCE

192.43mi

The Circuit Paul Ricard has been an off-and-on fixture in the Formula 1 calendar for more than 50 years.

It has been innovative, worn several hats and held a proud safety record for many years, but the French Grand Prix has used numerous circuits over the years, so Circuit Paul Ricard makes cameo appearances rather than regular slots in Formula 1.

The brainchild (and dream) of French business magnate Paul Ricard, the location is in the South of France, and just a 45-minute drive from the bustling port city of Marseille.

Ricard financed the project with his own money and wanted the circuit to be a state-of-the-art race track that was both fast and enjoyable. After purchasing a vacant tract of land near the small village of Signes, he employed the services of two of France's race legends in Henri Pescarolo and Jean-Pierre Beltoise to lend their expertise and knowledge to the design process.

With two long straights adjacent to each other, 15 turns and numerous chicanes, work began on the track at Le Castellet in 1969. It took 10 months to complete and was ready to host the 1971 French Grand Prix, which had first been held in 1906.

It was the first modern autodrome and possessed superb facilities for drivers, their teams and race fans, even if it didn't excite lovers of the thrills and spills classic road circuits of yesteryear.

In fact, drivers were largely unimpressed with the challenge Circuit Paul Ricard offered, though the expansive run-off areas gave them greater safety than perhaps any other track at the time.

The highlight of any drive, however, was undoubtedly enjoyed at Signes corner, at the end of the Mistral straight, and the rapid shift in speed and change of direction was an adrenaline rush that livened up a race that was occasionally described as 'perfunctory'.

Jackie Stewart would take the chequered flag in Circuit Paul Ricard's inaugural race, but in a nation of avid race fans, demand to host the event was fierce and tracks at Dijon and Charade shared Grand Prix duties until 1985 when Ricard's circuit enjoyed a seven-year unbroken spell as host of the international event.

The 1985 race proved to be an eventful one, with Keke Rosberg starting on pole in his Williams FW10. Despite going into the race after creating history at Silverstone, recording the fastest qualifying lap in Formula 1 history with a time of

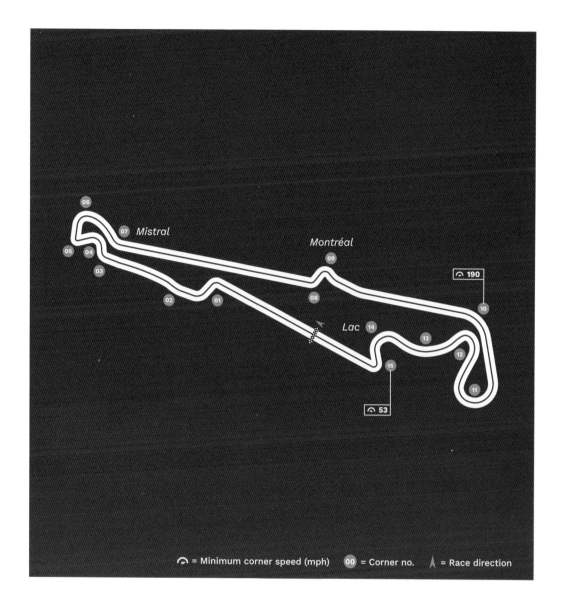

Mistral

Montréal

06
07
05
04
03
02
01
09
08
Lac
14
13
12
15
11
10

190

53

⌒ = Minimum corner speed (mph)   00 = Corner no.   ⅄ = Race direction

1:05.591 (until 2002 when the record was broken), the Finn would be bested at Circuit Paul Ricard by Nelson Piquet, who would take the chequered flag some 6.6 seconds ahead of Rosberg.

After the 1990 race, the French Grand Prix resided at Magny-Cours, leaving Circuit Paul Ricard to host various other motorsport events and a test track. It would be 30 years before Formula 1 would return.

With ownership passed to Bernie Ecclestone, it would spend time as a home to Toyota's Formula 1 team and was used for extensive testing for several years, before returning to the Formula 1 calendar as a race venue.

With an incredible 169 possible track variations, Circuit Paul Ricard was designed to be flexible, even if the vast majority of options are never used.

With no French Grand Prix held at all between 2008 and 2017 because of funding issues, Circuit Paul Ricard stepped in to revive the race in 2018 and were awarded a contract to host the event for the next five years, meaning Le Castellet was once again seeing Formula 1 action.

HUNGARY

Fernando Alonso
2003

BUDAPEST

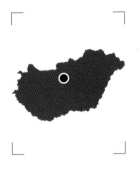

NUMBER OF LAPS
70

FIRST GRAND PRIX
1986

CIRCUIT LENGTH
2.722mi

RACE DISTANCE
190.53mi

Hungary's premier racing circuit, Hungaroring has been a permanent fixture on Formula 1's schedule since 1986.

With its numerous twists and tight turns, it is fair to say that it can be a difficult drive and not a favourite destination for many drivers – though the few that do enjoy it tend to thrive there.

Regardless of its layout, it is notable for being the first Formula 1 circuit to be included on the calendar in a nation that had once been behind the Iron Curtain.

It has undergone some cosmetic changes over time, the bulk of which were undertaken in 2003.

Racing in Hungary has been popular for many years, with the Budapest Grand Prix taking place on a street circuit in Népliget Park for several years in the 1930s, but when Eastern Bloc restrictions were eased and the country welcomed back visitors, a Formula 1 race was high on the wish-list of Hungarians and officials alike.

Though a Monaco-inspired street circuit at Népliget Park was mooted as a potential venue, plans were instead drawn up for a new track that the nation could take pride in and so land was acquired near Mogyoród that was deemed perfect for the construction of a track.

A little over 10 miles from the capital, it also had excellent transport links and the landscape was such that the track could be set in a natural bowl that would offer wonderful vantage points for spectators in numerous locations.

Ground was first broken on 1 October 1985 and would take just eight months to complete – quicker than any Formula 1 circuit had ever been laid out before – though plans were hastily amended when the discovery of an underground spring had to be negotiated and duly integrated into a tweaked layout.

By 1986, Hungaroring had successfully held several motorsport events and when Formula 1 came to the country, visitors flocked from neighbouring territories to see such a premium race in the flesh. Nelson Piquet took the chequered flag in the inaugural race in front of more than 200,000 fans. Formula 1 was here to stay.

In fact, in five of the first six Formula 1 years at Hungaroring, Brazilians stood first on the podium with Piquet winning again in 1987 and Ayrton Senna in 1988, 1991 and 1992.

With 11 wins for McLaren and seven wins for Williams, the British constructors dominate with a combined 18 victories, with Ferrari also on seven.

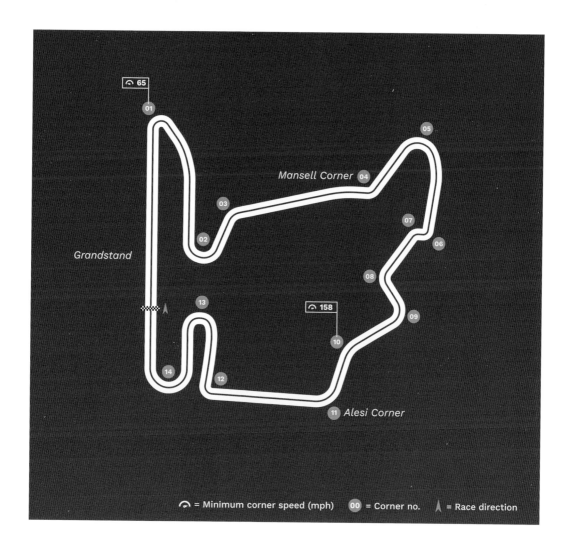

Mansell Corner

Grandstand

Alesi Corner

⌒ = Minimum corner speed (mph)   00 = Corner no.   ⋀ = Race direction

Consisting of 70 laps and a total distance of 2.722 miles (4.381km), the overall design proved to be something of an acquired taste – it was a difficult circuit, and the surface was more slippery than most tracks, making it a 'Marmite' ride that some loved and some hated.

Overtaking was difficult, with only the most skilled at being able to outmaneuver opponents resulting in successful passes. Nigel Mansell famously took advantage of Ayrton Senna's moment of hesitation in 1989 to expertly slip by and claim a dramatic victory.

Other notable races include the 2003 victory for Fernando Alonso in his Renault R23 – his only Hungarian success – after a faultless race that

saw him lap championship leader and world champion Michael Schumacher and finish 16.7 seconds ahead of second-placed Kimi Räikkönen.

Nobody has won the Hungarian Grand Prix more times than Lewis Hamilton who positively relishes the track, having won there no less than eight times – four more than Michael Schumacher who is in second place with four victories.

In the winter months of 2015-16, the entire surface was replaced at considerable cost, ensuring better grip for the cars' tyres along with tweaks at Turns 4 and 11.

Hungaroring may not have the glamour of Monaco, but it remains a good, solid destination for Formula 1.

BELGIUM

Damon Hill
1994

STAVELO

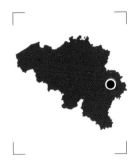

NUMBER OF LAPS	FIRST GRAND PRIX	CIRCUIT LENGTH	RACE DISTANCE
44	**1950**	**4.352mi**	**191.41mi**

The Circuit de Spa-Francorchamps in Belgium is an established Formula 1 circuit that has been a regular and favourite destination for more than 30 years.

Often simply called 'Spa', the first non-championship Grand Prix at the track was in 1925 and it has been host to many different motorsport races over the years.

As with many older circuits, it has undergone many changes, but the major redesign happened in 1979 when one of the world's longest race tracks was halved, going from 8.761 miles (14.100km) to 4.352 miles (7.004km) – effectively ending the use of public roads as part of the course and improving safety for drivers in the process.

Spa has always been one of the world's fastest circuits – much to the pride of the Belgians – but the original route, which used public roads as part of the design, was particularly dangerous with numerous potential hazards along the way including walls, trees, and telegraph poles.

These safety concerns added more than a hint of danger to racers, especially given the high speeds achievable to those willing to roll the dice.

It is that adrenaline rush that also makes Spa a track where drivers experience the true meaning of a Grand Prix more than perhaps anywhere else, with fast and challenging corners and the thrilling Eau Rouge sequence of corners an exhilarating section of the track.

The notorious Masta Kink section was regarded as the most difficult turn in the world, and the variable and unpredictable weather meant drivers could often be dealing with wet, slippery roads one minute, and dry surfaces the next. Sadly, the level of fatalities at Spa reached unpalatable levels for many.

Of course, even one death at a track is one too many, but Spa's list of deaths and casualties seemed to be out of control and the 1960 Belgian Grand Prix claimed the lives of two drivers within the space of just 15 minutes. Up to 2022, 23 drivers have died on the circuit.

Spa's reputation for being the most dangerous of all Formula 1 race tracks, with multiple accidents and deaths continued, resulting in some drivers skipping the event entirely. There were boycotts and race cancellations as drivers demanded the track be brought in line with the safety parameters at other venues.

As a result, after 1971, the Belgian Grand Prix was moved to other circuits and

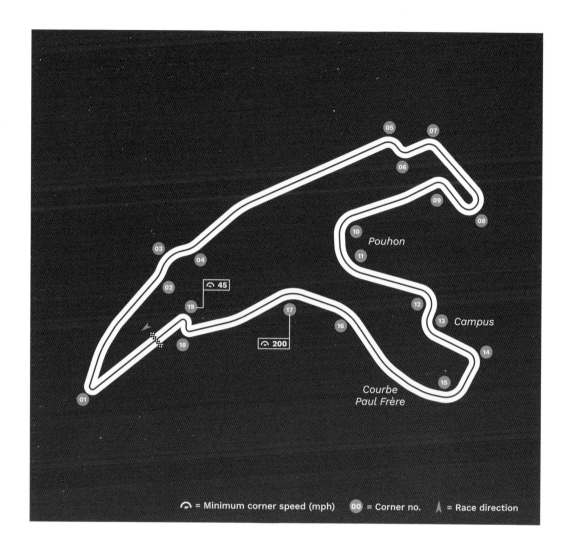

05 07 06 09 08 10 Pouhon 11 03 04 45 02 12 19 13 Campus 17 16 200 18 14 15 01 Courbe Paul Frère

= Minimum corner speed (mph)   00 = Corner no.   ⋀ = Race direction

would not return until 1983 and, with safety issues satisfied to acceptable levels, Spa was restored to the Formula 1 calendar and has been the host of the Belgian Grand Prix from 1985 until the present.

There have been many classic races and controversies at Spa, and 1994 proved to be one such example, with numerous incidents, collisions, and drama.

Michael Schumacher appeared to have extended his lead over the field as he raced home some 13 seconds ahead of Damon Hill, but excessive wear on the German driver's wooden skid block led to his disqualification and the victory was instead awarded to Hill in his Williams FW16B car.

Schumacher may have suffered in that race, but he still holds the most course wins (six), one ahead of Ayrton Senna's five wins at Spa. It is also a favoured track of Ferrari, who with 18 wins lead the constructors' table ahead of McLaren's 14.

There have been continual redesigns and safety improvements even up to recent years, due to the continued high rate of accidents.

Extensive plans to improve safety and carry on Spa's Formula 1 race venue status, unveiled in 2020, will take 10 years to complete and will cost close to £88.5 million (€100 million), almost certainly ensuring Spa remains on the Formula 1 calendar for the foreseeable future.

netherlands

Niki Lauda
1977

ZANDVOORT

NUMBER OF LAPS

72

FIRST GRAND PRIX

1952

CIRCUIT LENGTH

2.646mi

RACE DISTANCE

190.50mi

Set in the Dutch coastal town of Zandvoort, the circuit takes its name from its resort location, in the north of the Netherlands.

Opened in 1948 on the back of a swell in the popularity of motorsports that swept across post-War Europe, Zandvoort was a permanent track with public roadway sections and some of the track even dissecting the golden sand dunes of the town.

The brainchild of the Dutch Automobile Racing Club, former Le Mans champion Sammy Davis acted as sounding board and consultant when plans for the track were first drawn up.

It would be another four years before Formula 1 arrived and the inaugural 1952 Dutch Grand Prix was won by Alberto Ascari as Ferrari took all three spots on the podium.

It was the beginning of a 33-year run of Formula 1 races for Zandvoort that lasted until 1985. After that it would be another 35 years before Zandvoort saw Formula 1 action again.

One thing Zandvoort could never be accused of is being dull. A fast, sometimes hairy ride that is full of surprises, Zandvoort can accurately be

described as a rollercoaster of a ride. It has been the scene of many memorable moments and is a track where victory is often hard-earned and deservedly won.

But it has also not been without its dark moments, and the 1973 death of Roger Williamson was a tragic reminder of how dangerous the sport can be.

The British driver crashed and was trapped in his car and race marshals watched on while team-mate David Purley stopped his car and tried to rescue the stricken driver.

Poor communication and a failure to grasp the urgency of the situation meant Williamson ultimately died in an accident that may have been survivable and the race continued with other drivers unaware of the tragedy unfurling trackside.

The officials and the safety procedures at Zandvoort were severely criticised as a result, in one of Formula 1's most horrific incidents.

But it would be remiss to claim that this was a regular occurrence on a circuit that has proved incredibly popular over the years.

In 1977, Niki Lauda triumphed in his Ferrari 312T after a textbook race. Starting fourth on the grid, Lauda watched on as Mario

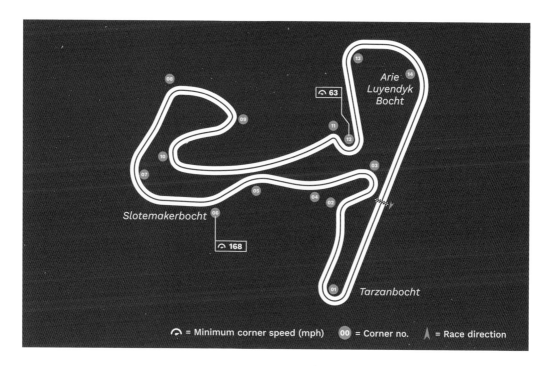

Arie Luyendyk Bocht

63

Slotemakerbocht

168

Tarzanbocht

= Minimum corner speed (mph)   00 = Corner no.   = Race direction

Andretti, Jacques Laffite and James Hunt aggressively fought for the lead in an explosive start. The destructive, petulant battle would see Hunt and Andretti's races both ended prematurely.

Lauda monitored it all from a safe distance, before gradually easing his way into the lead and from there he never looked back, holding off Laffite's challenge to extend his lead at the top of the Drivers' Championship.

Many other races told similar stories of drama and adrenaline-fuelled duelling. However, after the 1985 Grand Prix, the company that owned Zandvoort went bankrupt, and the circuit was taken off the schedule as a result.

The home of the Dutch Grand Prix fell into a steady decline, a large tract of land it had been on was sold for property development and there was no choice but to substantially shorten the track as a consequence.

The heady days of the Grand Prix it had once proudly hosted seemed a lifetime away.

In 1999, the circuit length was increased again, attracting some motorsport races back, but the circuit was mainly used as a training track for promising upcoming drivers.

Dutch Formula 1 fans would have to wait a further 21 years when, inspired by the emergence of Max Verstappen, interest in the sport reached fever pitch and the Netherlands once again demanded a race for their new national hero.

In 2020, Zandvoort returned to the Formula 1 schedule – how could the exciting talent of Verstappen not have a home Grand Prix? That same year the COVID-19 pandemic meant the homecoming race at Zandvoort was postponed. But in 2021, in front of an ecstatic and largely orange-coloured crowd, Verstappen won the first race back on the now 2.646 mile (4.259km) circuit, held over 72 laps.

Verstappen also won the 2022 Dutch Grand Prix to rubberstamp the return of Formula 1 in style – he'll need two more victories on home soil to equal Great Britain's Jim Clark who won the Dutch race four times, while Ferrari lead the constructors' table with eight victories at Zandvoort, which has made a welcome return for race fans worldwide.

ITALY

Phil Hill
1961

MONZA

NUMBER OF LAPS
53

FIRST GRAND PRIX
1950

CIRCUIT LENGTH
3.599mi

RACE DISTANCE
190.58mi

For many race enthusiasts, the mere mention of Monza is enough to send shivers of excitement down their spine.

The Autodromo Nazionale di Monza – or simply known as the Monza Circuit – is quintessential Formula 1, with mainland Europe's oldest track also being one of the most eagerly anticipated Grand Prix dates on the schedule.

Monza is not only one of the fastest circuits in the world, but also one of the largest, with a sprawling 3.599 miles (5.793km) distance stretched over 53 laps, traditionally the setting for a breathless spectacle from start to finish.

At Monza, dreams can sometimes be made, or, tragically, ended forever.

Bar one year when, in 1980, the venue was Imola, Monza has hosted Formula 1 since 1950 and was the third purpose-built racing track to be built, opening its doors for the first time in 1922 having taken just 110 days to create.

It staged the first Italian Grand Prix that same year and was the source of great pride for the people of Italy and put the Lombardy city of Monza on the map.

More than 3,500 men worked tirelessly to meet the deadline set by Grand Prix organisers, but they managed to complete it in time, with the hectic nature of its creation perhaps engrained in the very fabric of the track from its inception.

Monza is set in the Royal Villa of Monza Park, just north of Milan and the Formula 1 track – one of three on site – has held countless prestigious races over the years for a variety of motorsport disciplines.

For a time, Italy led the world with its Grand Prix, passion and cars, but it has also had its fair share of tragedy, perhaps no more so than the dreadful crash of 1928 when a car ploughed into the crowd and killed 28 spectators and the driver on a horrific day for Italian sport.

Improvements were made, but 14 more spectators were injured and three killed in a similar accident just three years later.

In 1933, three drivers lost their lives on the same day.

Thrills and excitement have always been high on the Monza agenda, but the increasingly faster cars started reaching dangerously high speeds after the track was extended in length in the 1950s and 1960s.

And tragedy still dogged this beloved track when a driver and 15 spectators

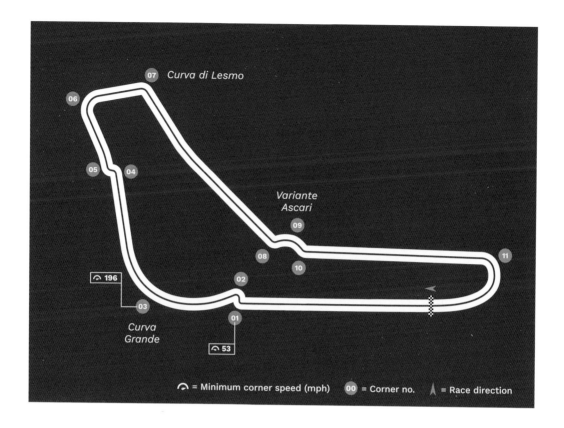

07 *Curva di Lesmo*

06

05 04

Variante Ascari

09

08

11

02

10

196

03

01

Curva Grande

53

= Minimum corner speed (mph)   00 = Corner no.   ⋀ = Race direction

lost their lives in a horrific crash in 1961.

American driver Phil Hill in his Ferrari 156 would win that race by more than 31 seconds, but when news of the tragedy in the stands filtered through, nobody was celebrating the victory in yet another dark day in Monza's history.

During the 1970s, Monza's thirst for speed was unsurpassed, with some of F1's most amazing finishes taking place on a track where it seemed everything was possible, all the way up to the chequered flag.

But at what cost?

It was decided that chicanes were needed to check expectations and reduce the danger this circuit, nicknamed 'The Temple of Speed', presented.

Yet, with more tweaks made to improve safety, Monza's reputation for incredibly fast races continued despite the fact that 52 drivers had lost their lives and 35 spectators

had also perished over the years.

Getting the balance of safety without diminishing the DNA of a Monza Grand Prix and the passion of the Italian fans – known as the 'tifoso', has been difficult for organisers.

But with each change came improved safety and in recent times, accidents and fatalities have been far fewer, though they still occasionally occur.

The early years were dominated by Italian drivers, but it is Lewis Hamilton and Michael Schumacher who have won more than any other driver at Monza, with five wins each.

Not surprisingly, an inspired Ferrari have won almost double the number of the next best constructor, with 20 wins to McLaren's 11.

Monza will continue to host the Italian Grand Prix for the foreseeable future.

Nico Rosberg
2016

SINGAPORE

Marina Bay Street Circuit

NUMBER OF LAPS
61

FIRST GRAND PRIX
2008

CIRCUIT LENGTH
3.146mi

RACE DISTANCE
191.82mi

The Marina Bay Circuit is one of Formula 1's new kids on the block.

Like Monaco and Valencia before it, Marina Bay is a street circuit set against spectacular Singapore skyscrapers and races for long stretches along a beautiful harbour.

It has all the glitz and glamour demanded of this elite motorsport event and was designed by the great Hermann Tilke with modifications made by KBR Inc.

It may have only appeared on the calendar in 2008, but it has quickly established itself as a firm favourite with drivers and fans alike.

The 3.146 mile (5.063km) circuit consists of 61 laps and its inaugural race created a piece of motorsport history when it became the first Formula 1 Grand Prix to be raced at night.

Around 1,600 bespoke floodlights were placed along the course and though they are up to four times brighter than the lights used at regular sports stadiums, they are designed to reduce glare as well as surface reflection to meet Formula 1 regulations and broadcast requirements.

The first race in 2008 was also the 800th World Championship race, marking another notable milestone in style, though the manner in which Fernando Alonso – who had begun 15th on the grid – eventually triumphed left a bad taste for many.

His Renault team-mate, Nelson Piquet Jr., deliberately crashed on lap 14, resulting in the safety car being deployed. This gave Alonso a much better chance of winning as he had gone into the pits before the safety car's arrival allowing him to resume as race leader and ultimately take the chequered flag.

As with other street circuits, Marina Bay is chock-full of tight corners – 23 in total – bends and numerous twists and turns, demanding high concentration and focus, making this a physically and mentally demanding drive.

And it is far from a smooth experience, with Marina Bay's bumpy roads and humidity being additional factors to deal with for the cars and drivers who can lose up to 3kg in bodyweight during the Grand Prix.

The section on Raffles Boulevard is particularly unforgiving and Lewis Hamilton claimed the track demanded double the concentration of the already-exhausting Monaco Grand Prix.

As a result of this continued issue,

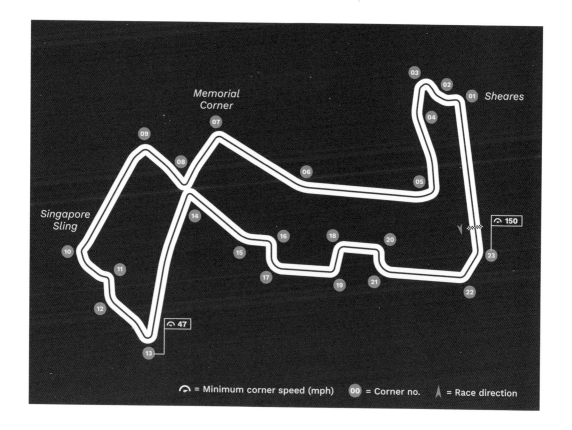

Memorial Corner

Sheares

Singapore Sling

150

47

⌒ = Minimum corner speed (mph)   00 = Corner no.   ⋀ = Race direction

work on upgrading the majority of the track's asphalt began in 2022.

Ingeniously designed, the Marina Bay Circuit has many notable features. Turn 18 gives race fans the unique experience of having Formula 1 cars speed beneath them with that part of the course passing underneath one of the grandstands!

Other landmarks include the Singapore Flyer, Parliament, the Supreme Court, City Hall and 112-year old Anderson Bridge.

The start and finish section of the track along with the pits and paddocks are permanent and purpose-built to host the race.

The Singapore Grand Prix was first held at Thompson Road from 1966 until 1973, before returning 35 years later at Marina Bay.

As with all circuits, tweaks have been made along the way, based on recommendations, complaints and

observations resulting in improvements that would make the race a more enjoyable experience. Further amends will be implemented for 2023, initially reducing the number of turns from 23 to 19, and shortening the overall distance.

Marina Bay's short run of consecutive Grand Prix races was halted in 2020 and 2021 due to the COVID-19 pandemic.

The popularity of the Singapore Grand Prix has remained high, but 2022 recorded the highest total attendance of 302,000.

Sebastian Vettel (with five wins) and Lewis Hamilton (with four) have dominated at Marina Bay over its first dozen races, with constructors Ferrari, Mercedes, and Red Bull all tied with four wins each.

Of the memorable battles there, Nico Rosberg's 2016 success is worthy of note, seeing off the challenge of team-mate Lewis Hamilton to mark his 200th Formula 1 race in style on his way to the World Championship.

JAPAN

Michael Schumacher
2002

MIE

Suzuka Circuit ●

NUMBER OF LAPS
53

FIRST GRAND PRIX
1987

CIRCUIT LENGTH
3.608mi

RACE DISTANCE
191.05mi

Initially designed in 1962 by Dutch race track designer John Hugenholtz, the iconic Suzuka International Racing Course – better known as the Suzuka Circuit – started life as a test track for Honda who financed the project.

The idea was to turn Honda into a manufacturing superpower and to have a track worthy of pushing their creations as hard and fast as they possibly could.

But what they had made was worthy of racing of the very highest standard, even if it took time to realise as much.

Based in Mie Prefecture, Japan, the classic layout Hugenholtz created is a figure-of-eight track, making it immediately familiar to children and adults who owned a Scalextric set at some stage in their lives, with its overpass section one of only two licenced by the FIA in world motorsport (the other being Ferrari's private testing track – the Fiorano Circuit – in Italy).

In 1976 and 1977, the first Japanese Grands Prix were held, both at the Fuji Speedway track, and thereafter it would be another 10 years before the event returned to the Formula 1 schedule.

It would be 25 years before Suzuka was put forward – and approved – to host a Formula 1 race, with

Gerhard Berger winning the first Formula 1 race there in 1987.

At 3.608 miles (5.807km) in length and a rapid 53 laps to the chequered flag, Suzuka is a challenging track to say the least, but a thrilling white-knuckle ride that is loved by all.

With capacity for 155,000 people, the track has been modified several times over the years, including mandatory changes to bring it up to Formula 1 standards which included tempering what had become an incredibly fast and, at times, dangerous circuit thanks to the introduction of various alterations and chicanes.

With its place on the Formula 1 calendar traditionally coming towards (or at) the end of the World Drivers' Championship, Suzuka has been the scene of some dramatic finales to the season and has had no less than 13 title deciders competed there.

With, more often than not, so much at stake, it is perhaps no surprise that the envelope is pushed so often at Suzuka, with drivers willing to take their cars to the absolute limit in search of glory.

From 1987 to 2007, Suzuka was the exclusive host of the Japanese Grand Prix and in 1994 and 1995, it became one of only nine Formula 1 circuits worldwide to

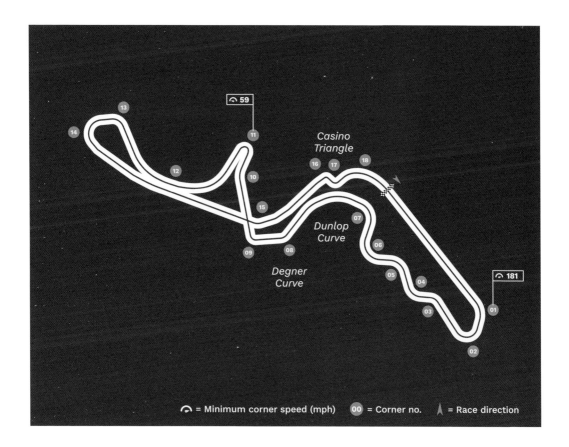

= Minimum corner speed (mph)　　00 = Corner no.　　↑ = Race direction

have hosted more than one Grand Prix inside the same season, when it briefly became home to the Pacific Grand Prix.

In 2007, the Japanese Grand Prix would move back to Fuji Speedway, owned by Honda rivals Toyota, after major improvements and modernization had been undertaken, and an agreement was put in place to share this prestigious event by alternating between Fuji and Suzuka each year.

However, the arrangement was short-lived with Toyota electing to withdraw from hosting the Japanese Grand Prix in 2009 due to the global economy taking a dip.

Suzuka happily stepped in and reinstated the Japanese Grand Prix, much to the delight of Formula 1 fans around the world.

One of Suzuka's darkest days came during the 2014 Grand Prix, when promising young French driver Jules Bianchi ran off the track in torrential

rain and horrifically crashed into a tractor removing another stricken car.

Though he somehow survived the impact, he died of his injuries several months later, leading to further safety recommendations in the aftermath of the accident.

There have also been many memorable races and climaxes to the season at Suzuka, and though the 2002 Grand Prix had little riding on it with the drivers' championship decided several races before, it showcased the brilliance of Michael Schumacher who gave a textbook race from the start to finish first in his Ferrari F2002.

It was one of six wins the German driver enjoyed in the Japanese Grand Prix – the most of any driver, with Lewis Hamilton close behind on five victories.

McLaren head the constructors' table with nine wins and Ferrari are next with seven.

USA

Max Verstappen
2022

AUSTIN

NUMBER OF LAPS

56

FIRST GRAND PRIX

2012

CIRCUIT LENGTH

3.425mi

RACE DISTANCE

191.63mi

It may have been the 10th host of the United States Grand Prix, but the Circuit of The Americas was the first purpose-built race track for Formula 1 in the USA.

Work first began in December 2010 and was completed almost two years later in October 2012, though it was beset by legal issues, funding disputes, expensive additional work, and other delays in what was far from a smooth journey from blueprint to reality.

Costing an estimated £247million ($300million), the track is located in Austin, Texas. The 3.425 mile (5.514km) track is home to Formula 1, NASCAR and the Motorcycle Grand Prix of The Americas as well as various other high-profile motorsport events.

It is an aesthetically pleasing and challenging circuit that is designed for speed – so much so the original name was intended to be 'Speed City'.

Like so many worldwide venues for Formula 1, the design was influenced by Hermann Tilke, though also conceived by a former motorcycle world champion (Kevin Schwartz) and a race promoter (Tavo Hellmund).

The United States Grand Prix has been running since 1908 but stopped in 1916 and would not take place again until 1958.

Resuming in '58, it ran for another 22 years – predominantly at Watkins Glen International – before taking another eight-year hiatus and re-emerging for three years at Phoenix.

The sporadic nature continued with no Formula 1 again from 1992 to 1999.

An eight-year stint at Indianapolis – five races being won by Michael Schumacher – took the USA Grand Prix to 2007 after which there was another four year gap.

And it was during that time that the Circuit of The Americas was completed and has been home to the race ever since.

Lewis Hamilton was the first driver to take the chequered flag in Austin, watched by an enthusiastic crowd of more than 100,000 who literally lapped up the 56-lap battle.

In fact, the British driver would win five of the first six races at the venue to move ahead of Schumacher as the most successful driver at the US Grand Prix.

Taking inspiration from some of Formula 1's most iconic tracks, the Circuit of The Americas has several features that pay homage to Silverstone,

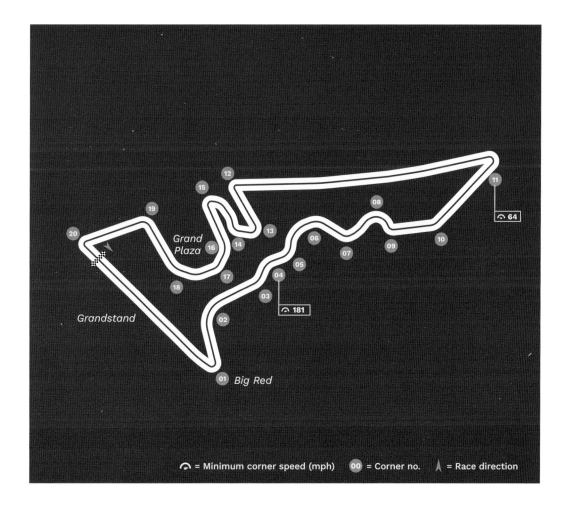

Grand
Plaza

Grandstand

Big Red

⌒ = Minimum corner speed (mph)   00 = Corner no.   ⋀ = Race direction

Suzuka and the Hockenheimring while maintaining its own look and feel.

Some areas of the track are sculpted into the contours of the land, and there are a number of wide corners which make for excellent overtaking opportunities.

Interestingly, it's one of only four Formula 1 circuits raced counter-clockwise – as the majority are clockwise – this means a lot more left-turns for drivers who are physically used to mostly right-hand turns so they have to adapt accordingly.

There are many unique features at the Circuit of The Americas, including a 251-foot (77 metre) observation tower, Grand Plaza, and Amphitheatre – to name but a few landmarks at this innovative and well-thought-out track.

Unfortunately, in a few short years, geological issues have caused problems, with the clay soil producing bumps where it has settled and dipped, and drainage issues causing flooding in 2015.

Resurfacing took place between 2019 and 2020, easing some of the problems, though not all, and a more substantial undertaking to repair worrying areas of the circuit began in January 2022. The results – which saw an epic battle between Max Verstappen and Lewis Hamilton in October of that year and saw the Dutch driver take the initiative of the Briton five laps from home to take the chequered flag in his Red Bull RB18 – were good enough to ensure this popular track will remain on the Formula 1 calendar until at least 2026.

MEXICO

John Surtees
1966

MEXICO CITY

Autódromo Hermanos Rodríguez

NUMBER OF LAPS

71

FIRST GRAND PRIX

1963

CIRCUIT LENGTH

2.674mi

RACE DISTANCE

189.73mi

Located in Mexico City, Mexico, the Autódromo Hermanos Rodríguez is named after brothers Pedro and Ricardo Rodríguez who were both tragically killed in crashes nine years apart – Ricardo on this circuit in 1962 and Pedro in Germany in 1971.

Hermanos Rodríguez sits within the boundaries of the Magdalena Mixhuca Sports City – a public, though largely undeveloped park located in the southeast of Mexico City.

The circuit, built in 1959 and based on the design of Hermann Tilke, was first used in 1962 for a non-Championship Grand Prix when it was known as the Magdalena Mixhuca, and it was during this race that local hero Ricardo Rodríguez was killed.

Despite the tragedy, a year later it held its first Mexican Grand Prix and would continue to do so for the next eight years, with British drivers enjoying great success with Jim Clark (three), John Surtees and Graham Hill taking the chequered flag in five of the first nine Formula 1 races there.

Surtees, driving his Cooper Maserati T81, won the 1966 race in what was his first victory for the Cooper Car Company. He held off the challenge of Jack Brabham to move up to second

in the Drivers' World Championship with an impressive performance.

Largely due to difficulties containing the vast crowds, the 1970 Grand Prix would be the last at the racetrack for some time. As some 250,000 packed the venue, barriers were torn down and (incredibly), crowds watched the race on the edge of the track itself! Crash barriers became vantage points and children even ran across the track in scenes that horrified Formula 1 officials. Because guarantees could not be satisfactorily made, it would not host Formula 1 again between 1971 and 1986, after which it reappeared on the schedule with the new name of Hermanos Rodriguez, and once again enjoyed a run of seven years of Grands Prixs.

Due to health and safety issues and a deteriorating surface, there was no Mexican Grand Prix from 1993 to 2014, despite the passion Mexican fans had for the sport.

In 2015, with a revamped track, every corner modified and much of the bumpy surface dug out and replaced, Hermanos Rodríguez returned to Formula 1 and has been a regular destination on the Formula 1 calendar, though with only 14 races to date, its race history is relatively brief.

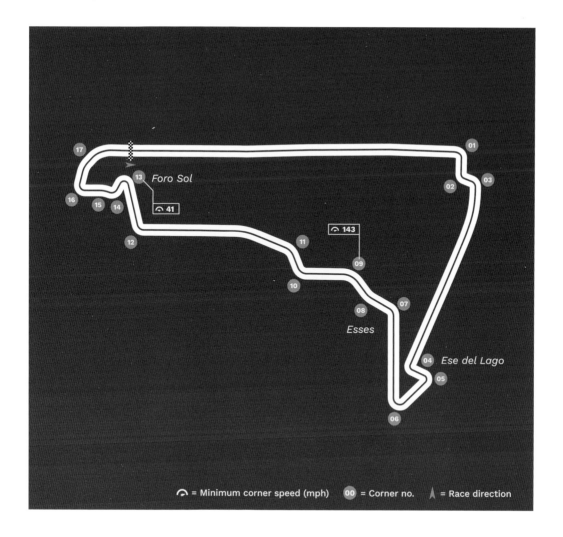

13 Foro Sol

⌒ 41

⌒ 143

11

09

10

08

07

Esses

04 Ese del Lago

05

06

17

16 15 14

12

01

02 03

⌒ = Minimum corner speed (mph)   00 = Corner no.   ▲ = Race direction

Measuring 2.674miles (4.304km) and raced over 71 laps, the circuit resembles the shape of a high-top baseball shoe and for a number of years was the location of the Formula 1 season finale.

It is also some 7,500 feet (2,205m) above sea level, giving it the highest elevation of any circuit in the world. The pollution issues of Mexico City make that, and the elevation, a problem for many teams and their cars.

Though the track today is different from the one first raced on in 1962, it remains faithful to much of the old route with one section memorably passing through the old Foro Sol baseball stadium, which is also the location for the podium

ceremony at the end with an atmosphere like nowhere else in Formula 1.

In recent years, Autódromo Hermanos Rodríguez has become a firm favourite of Max Verstappen, who – going into 2023 – had won four of the five previous races to become the most successful driver of the Mexican Grand Prix after easing past Jim Clark.

Lotus and Red Bull share top spot in constructors' successes there, with four victories each.

To recognise the support from local government, the 2022 Formula 1 race was renamed the Mexico City Grand Prix and it will host the event until at least 2025.

BRAZIL

Juan Pablo Montoya
2004

INTERLAGOS

Autódromo José Carlos Pace

NUMBER OF LAPS
71

FIRST GRAND PRIX
1973

CIRCUIT LENGTH
2.677mi

RACE DISTANCE
190.06mi

Situated between two large artificial lakes, Autódromo José Carlos Pace – located near the sprawling Brazilian metropolis that is São Paulo – is better known simply as 'Interlagos'.

The literal translation of Interlagos is 'between lakes' and it is here the country's premier Formula 1 circuit first came into existence in 1940.

Yet it wouldn't be until 1973 that the Brazilian Grand Prix was held there, with fever pitch scenes as Brazilian drivers won the first three races on the circuit.

Named after Brazilian Formula 1 driver Carlos Pace, who was killed in a plane crash in 1977, the 2.677 mile (4.309km) Interlagos was to enjoy only a brief spell of Formula 1 races, with safety concerns leading to driver protestations – predominantly because of the unacceptably bumpy surface.

Add in the deep ditches, embankments, and poor quality safety barriers, by 1980 Formula 1 organisers had seen enough, and the Brazilian Grand Prix was switched to Nelson Piquet's home town of Jacarepaguá where its one and only previous Grand Prix had been successfully held in 1978.

Jacarepaguá would host the event for the next nine years, with Piquet twice taking the chequered flag in front of an ecstatic home crowd.

But it was the emergence of a new Brazilian superstar that would lead to Interlagos making a spectacular return.

Ayrton Senna, arguably one of Formula 1's greatest drivers, was also one of São Paulo's favourite sons and had been crowned world champion in 1988.

The city demanded its hero be able to race on the circuit closest to his heart and – with an estimated £12.3million ($15million) revamp that reshaped, resurfaced, and shortened the track to make it a faster, more dynamic drive – in 1990 Interlagos returned to host the Brazil Grand Prix once again.

A year later, an ecstatic capacity crowd roared Senna to what would be his first victory on home soil.

Interlagos would host the Brazilian Grand Prix from 1990 onwards and in 2007, the troublesome asphalt surface that had continued to frustrate an otherwise thrilling circuit, was replaced entirely to give a much smoother drive, and encourage some truly thrilling battles.

One of the greatest races actually happened three years before the surface

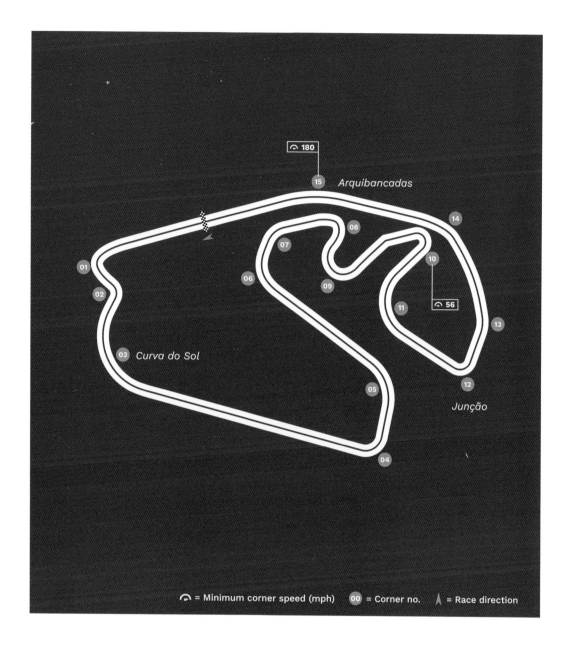

15 ⌒ 180

Arquibancadas

14

08

07

01

10

⌒ 56

02

06

09

11

03 Curva do Sol

13

05

12

Junção

04

⌒ = Minimum corner speed (mph)   00 = Corner no.   ▲ = Race direction

was replaced, with the final Grand Prix of the 2004 season not disappointing.

Though the championship had already been claimed by Michael Schumacher, Juan Pablo Montoya and Kimi Räikkönen served up a wonderful contest and if nothing else, the home fans could enjoy a South American triumph as Colombian Montoya, in his Williams-BMW car, took the chequered flag ahead of the Finnish driver, and local talent Rubens Barrichello took third.

Interlagos enjoyed an unbroken run of 29 years as Grand Prix host – with only the COVID cancellation of the 2020 race ending one of the longest continued runs of Formula 1 races at one venue.

It returned for 2021 and 2022 and it remains one of the most popular destinations for drivers and race fans alike, with the circuit that is located in 'The Land of the Drizzle' being anything but a damp squib.

UAE

Max Verstappen
2021

ABU DHABI

NUMBER OF LAPS	FIRST GRAND PRIX	CIRCUIT LENGTH	RACE DISTANCE
58	2009	3.281mi	190.25mi

Only the second Formula 1 race track built in the Middle East, the Yas Marina Circuit hosts the Abu Dhabi Grand Prix.

Yet another Hermann Tilke creation, the track is based on the man-made Yas Island in Abu Dhabi, the United Arab Emirates' capital and with a construction cost of approximately £825million ($1billion), that makes the UAE track the world's most expensive.

Work first began in 2007 and was completed in October 2009, just in time to host its first Grand Prix and become one of only a few venues to host a night race under floodlights.

The state-of-the-art track has 16 corners for drivers to master and numerous straights and the five grandstands allow for 60,000 spectators on race days.

When first used in a Grand Prix, the track received mixed reviews, with some drivers impressed and others distinctly underwhelmed.

Races thereafter have attracted criticism for being somewhat mundane, with few adrenaline rushes making for often disappointing contests, but like all Formula 1 circuits, it is constantly evolving and looking for ways to improve.

While its facilities – as you'd expect of an Emirate state – are second to none, the opportunities to overtake were few and far between, but in 2021, the track was reconfigured to overcome some of the flaws and make it less of a stop-start experience for drivers.

The inclusion of a banked corner at the southern end of the circuit has been widely praised and, in time, it's hoped that other improvements can make the race faster and more of a spectacle befitting of Formula 1.

The amends mean the race is shorter than when it first appeared on the schedule, with its 58 laps reduced to 3.281miles (5.281km).

The circuit is the centrepiece of some sizeable investment in Yas Island, where the grand plan had always been to turn the land into a tourist destination to rival the best on the planet.

With more than £32billion ($40billion) spent so far, Yas Island has delivered on its promise and what had previously been a largely blank canvas is now home to seven top hotels, a shopping mall, water park, golf course, concert venue, beach and a Ferrari indoor theme park adding to the glamour of having a Formula 1 festival once a year.

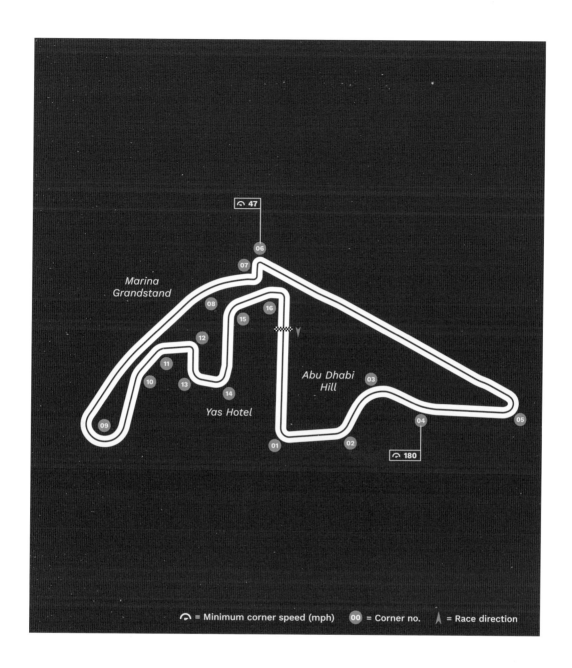

47

06

07

Marina
Grandstand

08

15   16

12

11

10   13

14

Abu Dhabi
Hill   03

Yas Hotel

09   05

01   02   04

180

= Minimum corner speed (mph)   00 = Corner no.   = Race direction

By the start of 2023, 14 Grands Prix had been held at Abu Dhabi with Lewis Hamilton winning five, and Max Verstappen and Sebastian Vettel taking three victories each.

Of those races, the 2021 battle will live long in the memory of those who witnessed it.

In the 2021 F1 finale, both Lewis Hamilton and Max Verstappen came into the race on 369.5 points each and for much of

that time, Hamilton looked set to claim a record eighth World Drivers' Championship.

But a dramatic final lap saw the Dutch driver overtake his great rival thanks to a controversial safety car in the final throes of the race. Mercedes complained long and loud, but their appeal fell on deaf ears and Verstappen's title was confirmed – despite race officials being proven to have misapplied regulations.

GERMANY

Jack Brabham
1966

RHINELAND-PALATINATE

Nürburgring

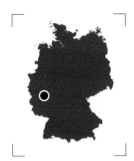

NUMBER OF LAPS

60

FIRST GRAND PRIX

1951

CIRCUIT LENGTH

3.198mi

RACE DISTANCE

191.76mi

Nürburgring first hosted the German Grand Prix in 1927 and, though not exclusively, it has continued to be part of the Formula 1 schedule up to the present day.

One of the longest tracks on the calendar, it is located in central Germany near the town of Nürburg, and sits among the Eifel mountains.

An at times undulating circuit, the north loop of Nürburgring sees an elevation shift of more than 300 metres (1,000 feet), not to mention the reported 170 corners, making this 150,000-capacity destination a challenging drive at the best of times.

The track's history is as long and colourful as the journey around it.

Work began in the autumn of 1925 and took 18 months to complete, designed by German architect Gustav Eichler.

To begin with, there were four track options – the Gesamtstrecke (Whole Course), Nordschleife (North Loop), Südschleife (South Loop) and Zielschleife (Finish Loop).

In its complete form, it was an enormous race track measuring some 17.4 miles (28km). The full circuit was used until 1929 when the Nordschleife version – slightly shorter – came into operation for the German Grand Prix.

Its first Formula 1 event was held in 1951 and would continue until 1954 – the horrific Le Mans disaster of 1955 saw many motorsport races cancelled following the deaths of one driver and 83 spectators, and the injuring of 180 more as flying debris from a crash resulted in tragedy.

Safety concerns meant many race tracks took immediate action and the German Grand Prix returned to Nürburgring from 1956 to 1959 before moving to Berlin for a year.

The Grand Prix returned to Nürburgring 12 months later and remained there for a decade, largely dominated by British drivers who recorded six victories at the circuit. Australian Jack Brabham, in his Brabham BT19 (1966), and New Zealander Denny Hulme (1967), winning twice at the circuit before Hockenheimring hosted the 1970 race.

Nürburgring resumed Formula 1 hosting duties for the next six years until it was the scene of Niki Lauda's 1976 horror crash, a shocking incident that perhaps further promoted the credentials of Hockenheimring as a major alternative venue.

The German Grand Prix moved back to Hockenheimring from 1977 to 1984 during which time the Nürburgring

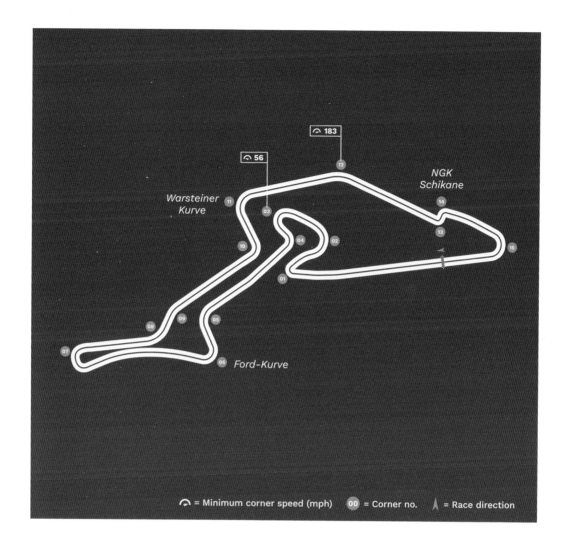

183

56

NGK
Schikane

Warsteiner
Kurve

Ford-Kurve

⌒ = Minimum corner speed (mph)   00 = Corner no.   ⋀ = Race direction

track underwent major reconstruction. The start/finish area was demolished, creating the new GP-Strecke version of the present day and though it returned to Nürburgring briefly in 1985, Hockenheimring became the dominant circuit for German motorsport, hosting the German Grand Prix from 1986 to 2008.

A deal was agreed to alternate the event between the country's two premier race tracks each year and in 2009, after an absence of 23 years, Formula 1 returned to Nürburgring.

However, under new ownership, the circuit was unable to fulfil its allotted biennial agreement and, as a result, the 2015 and 2017 German Grands Prix did not take place. But Nürburgring has proved a resilient venue. In 2020, it returned to host the Eifel Grand Prix – its fourth incarnation of Grands Prix following the German Grand Prix, Luxembourg Grand Prix and European Grand Prix which had all taken place there over time.

Whatever its future guise – German, Eifel, European or whatever, don't expect Nürburgring to disappear off the Formula 1 calendar – it is a circuit that, whatever problems beset it, always seems to find a way back into the hearts and minds of Formula 1 organisers.

Portugal

Ayrton Senna
1985

ESTORIL

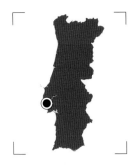

NUMBER OF LAPS
71

FIRST GRAND PRIX
1984

CIRCUIT LENGTH
2.725mi

RACE DISTANCE
193.47mi

The Circuito do Estoril or Autódromo do Estoril – or simply The Estoril Circuit, celebrated a half century of existence in 2022, though its somewhat chequered past means it has hosted Formula 1 only 13 times during that time.

Opened in 1972 and laid on a somewhat rocky plateau close to the coastal resort of Estoril, the people of Portugal had high hopes for the 45,000-capacity venue, but it would be beset by management issues and when it fell under the control of a military dictatorship, Estoril's future looked particularly bleak, and the circuit was left to gather dust as it was all but abandoned.

Formula 2 may have held races there, but Estoril had not come onto the radar of Formula 1 and looked unlikely to ever do so with tracks at Boavista and Monsanto sharing three World Championship races between 1958 and 1960.

Fortunately, the original vision for Estoril was realised when new owners financed much-needed repairs and refurbished the track in the early 1980s. In 1984 Estoril hosted its first Portuguese Grand Prix, with Alain Prost claiming the first chequered flag – though Niki Lauda's second place that day secured a dramatic World Championship win by just half a point.

The 1985 Grand Prix would be memorable for a number of reasons, but none more so than the peerless drive of 25 year-old Brazilian Ayrton Senna in his Lotus 97T. Senna's car led from pole to the finish line as he mastered the wet conditions to lap all but runner-up Italian Michele Alboreto, to record the first of his 41 Formula 1 victories. Those gathered that day knew they had witnessed something very special.

Estoril, though not the safest circuit in the world, became the scene of a number of memorable battles during its 13 years on the Formula 1 calendar and, as a result, a popular destination for drivers and teams.

Constructors Williams-Renault particularly enjoyed the track, with five of the last six races there ending in victory for them, and all with different drivers.

Alain Prost and Nigel Mansell have taken the chequered flag more than any other driver at Estoril, with three wins each.

However, demands from safety inspectors and Formula 1 officials for Estoril to carry out vital upgrades and improvements were met with empty promises and after a series of missed deadlines, the 1996 Grand Prix was the circuit's last.

02

03

167

05

04 Curva VIP

01

08

10

11 Esses

43

09

07

Gancho

12

06

13

⌒ = Minimum corner speed (mph)   00 = Corner no.   ⋏ = Race direction

In fact, the Portuguese Grand Prix disappeared off the schedule completely for the next 24 years until 2020 when it resurfaced at Portimão.

Estoril continues to host motorsport events and has done for many years, but whether the dream of once again hosting Formula 1 will ever be realised remains to be seen. Perhaps a future Portuguese Formula 1 superstar could help revive the fortunes of this once popular circuit.

SWE
DEN

Jody Scheckter
1976

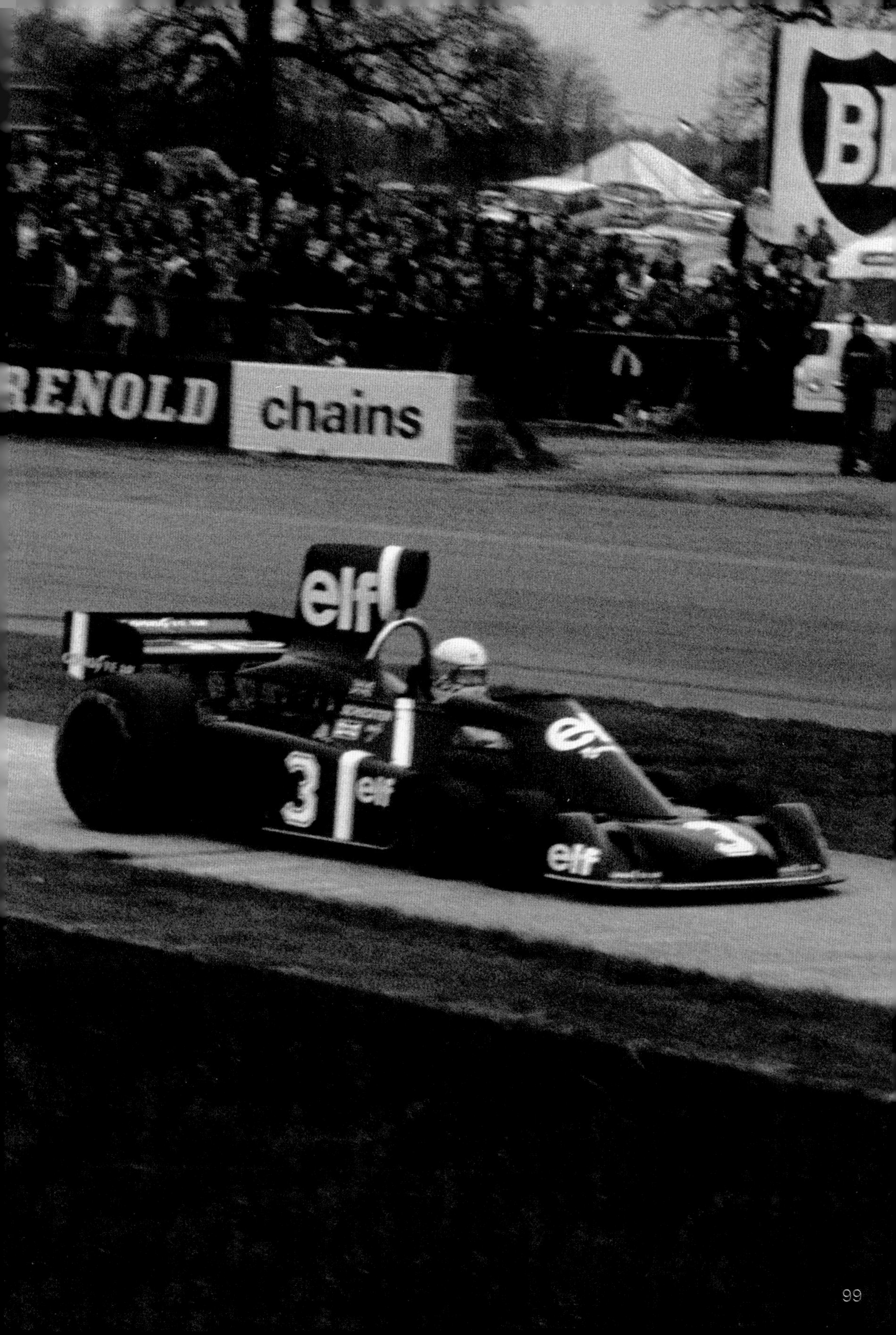

RENOLD
chains
elf
3
elf
elf
elf
3

ANDERSTORP

Anderstorp Raceway

NUMBER OF LAPS
70

FIRST GRAND PRIX
1973

CIRCUIT LENGTH
2.505mi

RACE DISTANCE
175.33mi

Scandinavia has sadly been an area of the world that has largely missed out on Formula 1.

Finnish champion Kimi Räikkönen has certainly done his bit for the sport in the Nordic region, but, for whatever reason, there is a distinct lack of top drivers hailing from the likes of Norway, Denmark and Sweden.

Sweden can at least claim some Formula 1 activity, albeit more than 45 years ago.

The Scandinavian Raceway – today known as the Anderstorp Raceway – was built in 1968 and quickly became a firm favourite among race fans and drivers alike.

Built on marshland near the small town of Anderstorp, designers incorporated a little-used airstrip into the circuit giving it a length of track known as the Flight Straight which continued to double up as a runway!

Buoyed by the success of Swedish driving stars Ronnie 'SuperSwede' Peterson and Gunnar Nilsson, Formula 1's arrival in Sweden was inevitable and the Scandinavian Raceway only sped up the process.

Eventually, in 1973, the first Swedish Grand Prix took place – there had been predecessors such as the Swedish Summer Grand Prix and other motorsport variants, but these weren't under the Formula 1 banner.

New Zealander Denny Hulme took the chequered flag for the inaugural race on the 2.501mile (4.025km) circuit.

Though the races at Anderstorp would be short-lived, they were rarely dull, and the 1976 Swedish Grand Prix illustrated this perfectly as South African Jody Scheckter took the chequered flag in his six-wheel Tyrrell P34 car!

The car was a sensation and caused reverberations in Formula 1, especially when Scheckter's team-mate Patrick Depailler made it a one-two on the podium for the six-wheeled curios.

However, they would be the only successes for the six-wheeled cars which disappeared from the sport almost as quickly as they had appeared.

But just six races into its Formula 1 life, Anderstorp was inadvertently hit by tragedy.

Few realised that when Niki Lauda crossed the line as winner of the 1978 Swedish Grand Prix, it would be the last Formula 1 race to be hosted there.

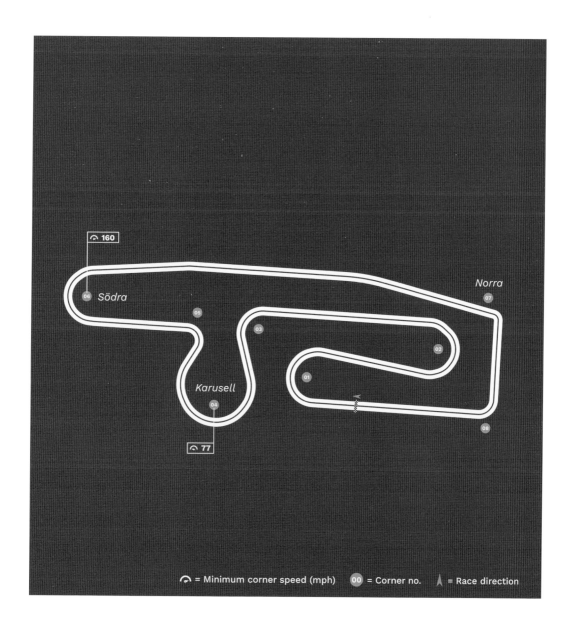

160

Södra · 06

05

03

02

Norra
07

Karusell

01

04

08

77

⌁ = Minimum corner speed (mph)   00 = Corner no.   ▲ = Race direction

That year proved a tragic one for Swedish motor racing as Formula 1 lost both Ronnie Peterson and Gunnar Nilsson.

Peterson died of complications from injuries sustained in September 1978 at Monza, aged only 34, and just over a month later, Nilsson succumbed to cancer and died in a London hospital aged just 29.

To lose two superstars so close together meant the Swedish public had no desire to see Formula 1 raced on its soil and there have been no Swedish Grands Prix held there since.

Anderstorp – which has largely remained the same since it was first built – continued to host motorsport in the years after, becoming a popular testing track for Swedish motor manufacturers and it continues to do so to the present day.

However, it seems unlikely there will be a return of the heady days of the mid-1970s when Sweden was firmly on the map and in the hearts of Formula 1 worldwide.

Argentina

Emerson Fittipaldi
1973

BUENOS AIRES

Autódromo Juan y Oscar Gálvez

NUMBER OF LAPS

72

FIRST GRAND PRIX

1953

CIRCUIT LENGTH

2.646mi

RACE DISTANCE

190.54mi

Opened in March 1952, the Autódromo de Buenos Aires Juan y Oscar Gálvez was the sole venue for the Argentine Grand Prix for 45 years before falling off the Formula 1 schedule completely.

Though motorsport was extremely popular in Argentina, races were exclusively on public roadways, and it took the interest and intervention of President Juan Perón to instigate the construction of a permanent track in the heart of the capital to really put Argentine racing on the world map.

The 45,000-capacity circuit, located in a Buenos Aires park in the south of the city, quickly established itself as one of the most versatile venues in motorsport. With its numerous track options to suit all manner of event, it is an attractive destination for numerous race meetings.

Though it has had several names over the years, it is today named after famous Argentine race brothers Juan and Oscar Alfredo Gálvez.

Built on a flat expanse of land, it has had various formats over the years and has been known as Buenos Aires No.2, No.9 and No.15, but the terrain of the area was marshy and caused some issues with the track surface. However, being completely level meant the 2.64 mile (4.259km)

race track could almost be viewed in its entirety from the extensive grandstands.

The first Argentine Grand Prix took place in 1953 and, though Italian driver Alberto Ascari took the inaugural chequered flag, it was a horrific crash that dominated the headlines after Giuseppe Farina lost control of his car which then ploughed into a group of spectators who had breached police lines to stand at the side of the track.

Nine were killed and 40 injured on a dark day for Argentine motorsport. But happier times were ahead for the South American nation, with local hero Juan Manuel Fangio winning the next four Grands Prix on home soil in front of ecstatic crowds.

Those heady days were soon forgotten, though, as government instability and financial problems meant there were no Grands Prix at all from 1961 to 1970, but it returned for five years from 1971 to 1975 on a twice-revised circuit. Though there were no Argentinian successes, Emerson Fittipaldi became the first Brazilian to win on Argentine soil in his Lotus 72 in 1973, and he repeated the feat in 1975.

There was no race in 1976 but the Grand Prix continued in 1977 until 1981 when the Argentine invasion of the British

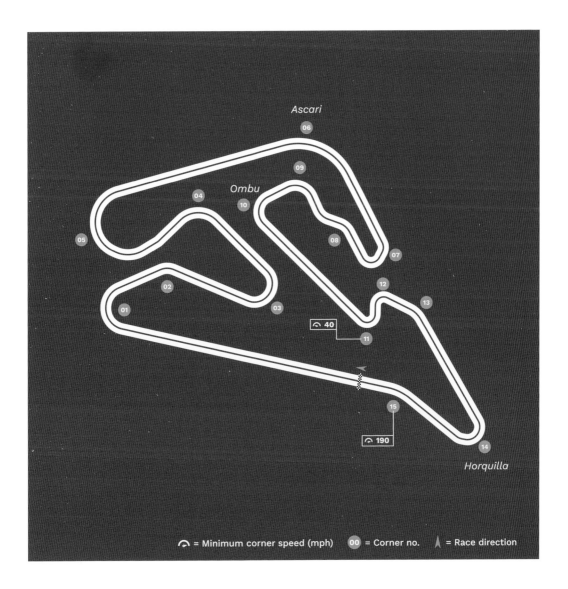

Ascari
06
09
Ombu
04
10
05
08
07
02
12
01
03
13
🔄 40
11
15
🔄 190
14
Horquilla

🔄 = Minimum corner speed (mph)   00 = Corner no.   ⋀ = Race direction

colony of the Falkland Islands saw the Argentine Grand Prix removed from the Formula 1 calendar indefinitely.

Ironically, when the race resumed in 1995, it was won by British driver Damon Hill, who repeated the feat the following year, but by that time hostilities between Argentina and Britain had calmed considerably.

Financial issues again beset the circuit and the 1998 Grand Prix was the last for the Autódromo de Buenos Aires Juan y Oscar Gálvez, which hasn't been part of the Formula 1 calendar since.

Several attempts have been made to revive the Argentine Grand Prix and though negotiations have consistently fallen through, there is a desire from all parties to see it return to the schedule at some point in the not-too-distant future.

Fittingly, nobody has won more races at the circuit than Argentina's favourite racing son, Juan Manuel Fangio, whose four successes there are likely to remain a record for many years to come.

SOUTH
AFRICA

Jim Clark
1965

CAPE PROVINCE

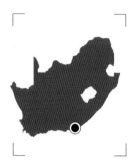

NUMBER OF LAPS
60

FIRST GRAND PRIX
1962

CIRCUIT LENGTH
2.436mi

RACE DISTANCE
145.76mi

South Africa's oldest race track, the Prince George Circuit is located near the coastal city of East London in South Africa's Eastern Cape Province.

It first held a major race in 1934 and proved extremely popular with race fans, attracting huge crowds of 60,000-plus on a route that was fast and furious and a number of cars achieved record speeds.

It was part street circuit and part permanent track – the latter being predominant today – with fast corners and an epic stretch that ran along the shores of the Indian Ocean. It was originally an enormous and picturesque circuit that spanned 15.199 miles (24.461km).

So successful and thrilling were the non-championship events that it was only a matter of time before Prince George became part of the Formula 1 World Championship and, finally, in 1962 it did.

Ironically, modifications to make the track suitable for Formula 1 in 1959 were actually the beginning of the end for the Prince George Circuit, which was dramatically redesigned and cut in length to just 2.436 miles (3.920km), and after just three South African Grands Prix, it was deemed too small for Formula 1 racing!

After the inaugural Formula 1 South African Grand Prix, Prince George Circuit would host just two more Grands Prix – with all three won by British drivers – before being relocated to the larger purpose-built Kyalami Grand Prix Circuit near Johannesburg.

The final Formula 1 race at Prince George on New Year's Day 1965 was suitably thrilling, with Jim Clark taking the chequered flag in his Lotus Climax some 30 seconds faster than John Surtees to start the season off in style. British drivers took the first four positions that day, with Graham Hill third and Mike Spence fourth.

Though there was a Grand Prix at East London in 1966, it wasn't part of the World Championship.

Kyalami Circuit took the reins from 1967 until 1993 (save for a seven-year gap due to Apartheid and a worldwide ban on sport in South Africa).

But write off the Prince George Circuit at your peril.

A 20-year lease was agreed with the Border Motorsport Club in 2014 with plans announced for a £33million ($40.1million)

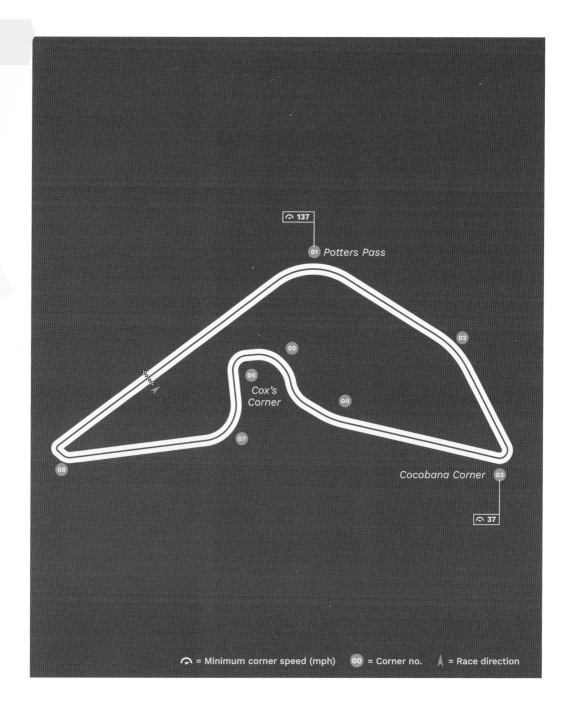

01 *Potters Pass* — 137

02

05

06 *Cox's Corner*

04

07

08

Cocobana Corner 03 — 37

= Minimum corner speed (mph)   00 = Corner no.   = Race direction

redevelopment to bring the circuit back up to international standards.

This will include a revamped circuit, new pits and lanes, a media centre, new grandstands, a new medical facility and a luxury oceanside hotel.

The South African Grand Prix – not held since 1993 – may yet re-emerge in East London...

Other Titles in this Aspen Books Series include:

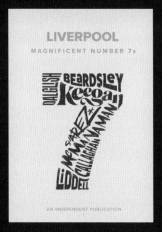

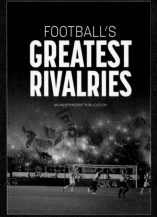

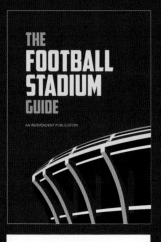

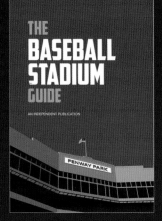

www.aspenbooks.co.uk

FORMULA ONE ICONS

Written by David Clayton
Designed by Daniel Brawn

ASPEN
BOOKS

© 2023. Published by Aspen Books, an imprint of Pillar Box Red Publishing Ltd. Printed in India.

ISBN: 978-1-914536-73-1
Images © Alamy